KT-484-309

ROCK CLIMBING

INTRODUCTION TO
ESSENTIAL TECHNICAL SKILLS
FOR LEADERS AND SECONDS

by

Pete Hill MIC, FRGS

NORWICH CITY COLLEGE		
Stock No.	252844	
Class	796.5223 HIL	
Cat.	NH	Proc	3WL

2 POLICE SQUARE, MILNTHORPE, CUMBRIA, LA7 7PY
www.cicerone.co.uk

© Pete Hill 2007
ISBN 13: 978-1-85284-529-2
Reprinted 2008 (with updates)

A catalogue record for this book is available from the British Library.

To my parents, for putting up with it all over the years!

ACKNOWLEDGEMENTS

As always, I'm indebted to friends, acquaintances and others who have eased the passage of this project through their unselfish help and support. Chris Pretty gets the blame for the original idea for this book, and it is down to him that my family has hardly seen me for a few months. Jonathan Preston and Rob Johnson kindly let me use some of their climbing photographs, and my thanks go to them. Rebecca and Samantha Hill unflinchingly assisted with belaying and climbing for some of the photographs, and both deserve my gratitude. James Hotchkiss helped with a huge photo session on a particularly raw December day, so in the absence of a medal he will have to do with my heartfelt appreciation.

Equipment support was generously supplied by a number of companies, with particular thanks to Frank Bennett at Lyon Equipment (www.lyon.co.uk), Beal for the ropes and software (www.bealplanet.com), Petzl for various hardware (www.petzl.com), DMM for technical hardware such as wires and cams (www.dmmclimbing.com) and La Sportiva (www.lasportiva.com) for rock shoes.

Finally, Paula Griffin once again burnt the midnight oil trying to make sense of my often illegible scratchings, as well taking part in many photographic sessions, and for that – as well as being the perfect climbing partner – I am eternally grateful.

NOTE
To avoid confusion when describing sequences of moves the use of 'they' has been avoided. Where appropriate, the pronouns 'he', 'him' and 'his' are used to refer to both male and female climbers and seconds.

DISCLAIMER
Whilst every effort has been made to ensure that the instructions and techniques in this book cover the subject safely and in full detail, the author and publishers cannot accept any responsibility for any accident, injury, loss or damage sustained while following any of the techniques described.

Front cover: Jonathan Preston on 'Probe', E1 5b, Creag Dubh in northern Scotland

ROCK CLIMBING

INTRODUCTION TO
ESSENTIAL TECHNICAL SKILLS
FOR LEADERS AND SECONDS

252 844

ABOUT THE AUTHOR

Pete Hill MIC, FRGS has climbed in many continents and countries across the world, including first ascents in the Himalayas. He is a holder of the MIC award, the top UK instructional qualification, and has been delivering rock and mountain sports courses at the highest level for a number of years. He is a member of the Alpine Club, honorary life member of the Association of Mountaineering Instructors and a Fellow of the Royal Geographical Society. A lack of common sense has caused him to be found on the north faces of the Eiger and Matterhorn in winter, as well as on a number of other extreme routes climbed in difficult conditions in the European Alps, Africa, Nepal and India.

Pete lives in Scotland and has two daughters, Rebecca and Samantha. A frequent contributor to various magazines and websites, he is also author of *The International Handbook of Technical Mountaineering* and *Sport Climbing*, and co-author (with Stuart Johnston) of the globally successful *The Mountain Skills Training Handbook*. He runs both summer and winter skills courses from beginner through to advanced level, and can be contacted via his website at www.petehillmic.com.

CONTENTS

'Fingerwrecker', HVS 5c – steep granite climbing at the Pass of Ballater

INTRODUCTION

This book is aimed, quite simply, at anyone who wishes to climb. Although billed as an introduction to rock climbing, it will be relevant for anyone who wishes to extend or improve his or her technical skills for single- or multi-pitch routes, whether wanting to second, lead or top-rope.

Rock climbing has become a huge participation sport, and the number of people taking to the crags increases substantially every year. Many climbers – including me – were initially self-taught; some have been mentored by friends; a few will have learnt their skills on a formally instructed climbing course. The intention of this book is that the techniques described will appeal to everyone who likes to climb, enabling the reader to learn new skills or to consolidate those already acquired. The chapter order, moving from basics through to skills – such as ropework and runner placement – and finally to climbing, leads the novice in a logical progression. Individual sections can be referred to as and when necessary. Several chapters cover subjects or techniques that can be practised at home, such as those on knots and the mechanics of belaying.

The book will also prove a handy reference for anyone starting out and being mentored by another climber, as it clearly demonstrates current best practice in a number of the disciplines. This is essential if you are going to be able to tie on, belay and second effectively, paving the way to learning more as you progress through the grades. Many people are introduced to climbing by a friend, and most will enjoy the experience to the extent that they will want to take it further. Leading a route is often the main focus, and it is useful to have written information to hand on the most important aspects of gear placement and on

how to adjust your mind to the leading process. There is, of course, nothing to compare with getting out on the crag and practising for yourself; even better if this can be done in conjunction with an experienced friend and a good work of reference.

A good number of climbers take up the sport after attending sessions at a climbing wall, and will often be capable of climbing to a high grade indoors. This book covers all the skills required for a safe transition to climbing in the outdoors. It is very unusual for someone who is capable of climbing, say, 5c indoors to climb anywhere near that grade outside initially. This is due to a number of factors. On a climbing wall it is easy to spot the next hold, work out how to get there and proceed up with the minimum of fuss – as long as the hold is any good! However, outside there is no colour coding of the rock, and as a consequence finding holds will take a lot longer. We cannot just launch up and reach for whatever is obvious – it may be just a sloping ledge or a blind pocket. We must take time to look around for holds and try some out, searching with our hand whilst holding ourselves in balance, before deciding on which one to use.

The process of finding suitable holds outdoors – which takes around five times longer than on a climbing wall – usually means that the technical difficulty of the route will go down. If it takes six minutes to climb a route indoors it may take as long as thirty minutes outdoors. You will get more tired on the longer route, and your overall grade will tend to be lower than you are used to. This does not matter, however, and I would encourage everyone to climb easy grades until they are happy and safe before progressing up the grade scale.

Placing gear on the lead

It is interesting to note that a good number of people attending climbing courses have climbed in the past and stopped, often quite a long time ago, then decide to take up the sport again. Usually this seems to be down to family commitments, or another diversion such as working abroad. Such people tend to choose an instructional course in order to get back up to speed. Those who, perhaps, don't wish to go on a course will also find this book invaluable. The information contained herein will act as a prompt to those previously learned techniques that may have become a little rusty. Current best practices will also be observed, as techniques, equipment and views may have changed over the intervening years.

Courses are an excellent way of learning the basics from scratch, or for progressing through to intermediate or even advanced level. Attending a well-run, low-ratio course with a qualified instructor is the best way to learn the skills necessary to keep you safe and to give you an enjoyable time climbing rock. Referring to a good reference book long after the course has finished will be good revision of the course content. It is easy to attend a number of sessions with an instructor and feel swamped with information; such a book will help you to sort out the wood from the trees. Photographs and the presentation of various ideas and tips on how to get the job done effectively and safely will further consolidate the lessons learnt. Taking notes during the course is a very good idea, as these can be cross-referenced with the book and a satisfactory answer to technical questions easily found.

Parenthood results in a lot of wrinkles! I have two daughters and will always try to take an interest in what they do. They both enjoy climbing, and have been able to benefit from my experience and to learn various climbing skills in a safe and appropriate manner. Concerned non-climbing parents often ask me how best to tackle the fact that their son or daughter has taken up the sport and seems to be enjoying it.

Obviously, the answer will be to encourage them as much as possible, and see to their outdoor safety needs by sending them on a suitable course or out with experienced friends who can teach them what they need to know. When this is impossible – perhaps the family has no climbing contacts – some parents take it on themselves to learn the skills, with the intention of then teaching their offspring. Simply having the ability to arrange a safe top or bottom rope not only means that the son or daughter can climb safely, but also opens up a whole new realm of joint activities for the family at weekends or on holidays. Everyone wins: the parent wins as they have a grasp on what their son or daughter is getting up to on the crag; the child wins as they get safe conduct and tuition; the family as a whole wins as all members take part in a challenging sport together.

Climbing, in all its forms, takes time to learn properly. Obtaining experience is essential in progressing through the grades and technicalities that make this sport so challenging. Make sure that you work out a sequence of skill development that suits your aims and aspirations. If you are new to climbing, for instance, wanting to lead from day one will not be a good idea. Building up a solid base of seconding experience would be the way ahead, and consolidating the knowledge learnt before getting on to the 'sharp end' of the rope yourself.

So – you have seconded, led, climbed multi-pitch routes and abseiled back down, all very safely. What next? Building up a base of experience will be essential to becoming a safe, all-round rock climber. Sometimes you may need that little extra 'something' to help maintain your interest but also to enhance your own knowledge and help you progress further. Attending a course will be one way of doing this, providing you ensure that the instructor is qualified to the correct standard. A well-run course will often be on a 1:1 or 1:2 basis, allowing you plenty of time to learn and practise the skills that are demonstrated in a very controlled manner.

Watching DVDs can also help you make progress (although they can never match the benefits of the 'personal touch'). However, the information they contain can recall forgotten skills, and if well made will inspire you to get out on the rock. There are a few instructional DVDs available, together with a myriad of global bouldering

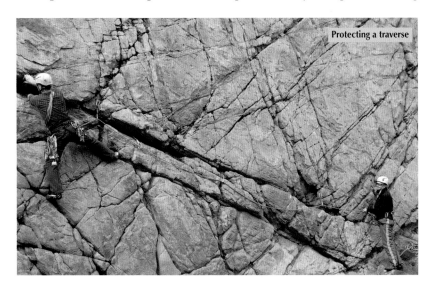

Protecting a traverse

and hard-rock-climbing 'pump-fests'. The latter will either supply you with lashings of intent, or merely deflate you as you see climbers in need of a good meal gracefully elevating themselves across seemingly hold-less terrain, often upside down, on sun-kissed rock in beautiful locations around the world!

Maintaining personal fitness – climbing and general – is also important. Diet becomes a consideration when climbing at the higher levels, but fitness training is relevant to everyone, and essential if you wish to progress through the grades. Several books give advice on the best way to train, and sessions are available at climbing walls and with individual instructors. Nutritional information can be accessed through publications and via the Internet. A visit to a climbing wall during the winter months, or whenever there is an enforced lay-off due to bad weather, will help to keep your climbing fitness levels high. It is also a great way to meet people and make contacts, useful for finding partners and arranging car-shares to more distant crags.

If you are interested in taking your climbing forward, you may like to work towards a formal qualification. A very pop-ular award in the UK is the Single Pitch Award (SPA), which trains and assesses candidates at a level of competence based on a well laid-out syllabus, and looks at personal skills as well as those needed for taking others climbing and abseiling. As there is no formal requirement in the UK for such a qualification when taking people climbing, many who go through the SPA process do so for their own personal benefit and to get themselves assessed at the national standard – a great boost to their confidence. Other countries around the world have similar schemes, and details of these can be obtained from their relevant mountaineering governing bodies.

I hope that you find the contents of this book useful. Although it covers many techniques, you will probably come across alternatives when climbing with other people. Make sure that the skills demonstrated are both safe and relevant to you and your style of climbing, and beware of 'quick fixes' which may appear to save time but may be either inappropriate or just downright dangerous. If in doubt, stick to what you know.

Above all – be safe and have fun.

Sandstone climbing on 'Centre',
Mild VS 4b, Cummingston

1 GETTING STARTED

Understanding guidebooks and grades can be one of the most daunting aspects of going out climbing. If you can decipher 'guidebook speak', and have an idea of how the grading system works, you will have mastered one of the hardest parts of your day at the crag! It takes time to learn how to relate the descriptions and drawings in the guidebook to the rock in front of you, but a little time and perseverance will pay dividends.

UNDERSTANDING GUIDEBOOKS
One of the joys of a good guidebook is that you can sit at home and work out in advance almost every detail of the route that you are going to climb. You'll know where to park, how to get to the crag and how long the climb will take. There'll be information about the different sections, which routes are where and the relevant grades. There will probably be a 'topo', a topographical diagram of the cliff with lines depicting the route. Descents are also regularly described when not obvious, as will key crag features such as prominent trees, rock features and the like. Most guidebooks will also contain a number of inspiring photographs, designed to make you want to rush out there and get going!

A typical guidebook will cover a number of crags in a geographical area, the clue being in the title: 'Swanage and Portland' or 'The Ogwen Valley', for example. Decide where you want to go, then find a copy of the relevant guidebook in a climbing shop or via the Internet. Inside the book cover there will often be a rough sketch map of the area with the crags marked, along with any relevant towns or other features. The first few pages will contain a general description of the site, access, history and so on. The crags will then be listed, either alphabetically or grouped by location. Each chapter will detail where the crag is, how to get there and where to park, plus a bit about its character and any access issues.

An assortment of guidebooks

The routes will be listed in a logical manner, although this section may be a little confusing at first. On a small single-pitch crag the climbs will commonly be described starting from either right or left, or perhaps from an obvious feature such as a huge oak tree in the centre. Anything else noteworthy on the crag will be mentioned, and this can help you get your bearings. For instance, there may be a large corner and a route description telling you to start '3 metres to the right', leaving no doubt as to where the climb is.

Where crags have a number of buttresses, these will often be described in the sequence in which you approach them from the parking and access point. A time may be given for the walk to each section (although this tends to be very subjective). Obvious features will be mentioned, and the topos will also usually give a clue as how the sections relate to each other.

Multi-pitch crags should be looked at from a different aspect (literally). With a single-pitch route you can probably get all the information you need by standing at the bottom and looking up it. A crag with a series of long routes on it will, by definition, be high, so stop some distance from it and, using the guidebook and your own observations, pick out relevant features. Chimneys, crack lines, overhangs and similar formations should all be discernible from a distance, and you can then relate these to the description of your chosen route in the book.

CHOICE OF ROUTE

You will probably have decided, well before arriving at the venue, which route or routes you intend to do. An ideal route on a single-pitch crag – if one exists – will include the following features:

- Ease of access.
- Flat, clean base at the bottom of the climb.
- Safe and suitable gearing-up area.
- No mass of people queuing to get on it.
- Should look appealing.
- Rock will be dry and the weather lovely.
- Opportunity for ground anchors.
- Plenty of cracks and so on for gear placements.
- Selection of good anchors at the top.
- Belay position for the leader will allow good line of sight and communication with the second.
- No objective danger, such as loose rocks.
- Descent will be a simple walk off.
- Many similarly perfect routes very near by.

Note

The first ascensionist names and grades the route. The grade will usually be about right and will be accepted straight away by other climbers. However, sometimes routes have been under- or over-graded at the outset, seeming harder or easier than you thought. Such discrepancies will be corrected over time, and subsequent guidebooks will show the revised grade.

The top of the appropriately named 'Gorse Route'!

Perhaps there aren't that many routes like this around – but you will be surprised just how many of these criteria can be met at a good venue.

A lot of guidebook compilers will use a star rating, often ranging from one to three. These are only applied to those routes that, in the opinion of the author, merit special mention. Although this is a good way to highlight climbs that might be worth seeking out, bear in mind that this is the author's idea of a good route, which may not be the same as yours. Also, a route with no stars is not necessarily a poor climb, and may suit your particular style or aspirations perfectly. Conversely, a three-star route may not impress you in the slightest. Use this system as a guideline; at the end of the day deciding what to climb will be down to you.

FINDING YOUR ROUTE

As mentioned above, obvious features such as chimneys, trees and so on will be used as reference points when locating a particular route. However, if you are still having trouble finding a climb, use the information at the start of the route description to help. For instance, it may be graded at 'V. Diff' (see below), at the easier end of the scale. If the piece of rock you are looking at is smooth and devoid of any holds you are obviously in the wrong place. Use the length of the route – normally given at the start of the description – to help. If the climb is described as being 5m, but the section of rock you are looking at goes up for 30m, that again must be the wrong one.

Check the route description too. A blank-looking slab in front of you with the route line being described as 'take the obvious chimney' should set off alarm bells.

The name of the route can sometimes help. Titles such as 'Classic Crack' or 'First Corner' are obvious indicators. Be aware, though, that the person who first named them may have had a warped sense of humour, and called a route 'slab climb' when it is in fact a greasy chimney. Not very common – but misleading nonetheless.

GRADES

You need to have a little climbing under your belt before you can start to get an appreciation of what the grading system means and at which level you are comfortable climbing. It seems to be a mass of letters and numbers at first, but will make sense to you before too long. The table below gives an indication of how these figures fit together.

UK SERIOUSNESS	UK TECHNICAL
Easy	–
Moderate	–
Difficult	**3a**
Very Difficult	3a, **3b**
Hard Very Difficult	3b, **3c**
Mild Severe	3c, **4a**
Severe	**4a**, 4b
Hard Severe	4, **4b**, 4c
Mild Very Severe	**4b**, 4c
Very Severe	4b, **4c**, 5a
Hard Very Severe	**5a**, 5b
E1	5a, **5b**, 5c
E2	5b, **5c**, 6a
E3	5c, **6a**, 6b
E4	**6b**, 6c
E5	6b, **6c**
E6	6c, 7a
E7	6c, 7a, 7b
E8	6c, 7a, 7b, 7c
E9	7a, 7b, 7c, 8a
E10	7b, 7c, 8a
E11	7b, 7c, 8a etc

The left-hand column shows how 'serious' a climb is going to be; it can be used as an indicator as to how much protection there is on the route and how sustained it is. This is sometimes known as the 'adjectival' grade. The right-hand column shows the technical grade, which indicates the difficulty of the hardest move or sequence of moves. Combining these two together will give a lot of information about a climb. Note that routes below 'Difficult' standard, and often those below 'Severe' standard, are not often given a technical grading as it is felt that the adjectival grade gives enough information at that level.

As you progress through the grades you will need to know how they fit together. Each of the higher grades, from 'Severe' upwards, has a 'benchmark' grade. This is a degree of seriousness and technical difficulty that can be seen to be an average given that level of climbing. These benchmarks are given in bold type on the table above.

Note

Anyone starting to climb outdoors after a few sessions on a climbing wall will find that the grades feel different to those used indoors. As a general guideline, indoor grades, which are based on French sport grades, tend to be about two steps 'up' from the UK outdoor grades. Thus, a climbing wall grade 5 would be about 4a outside.

For instance, Very Severe (VS) 4c is a benchmark grade, where the seriousness and the technical difficulty are what you would expect at that level of climbing. However, there can be considerable variation within this. An example would be a route graded at VS 5a. This means that the technical grade is harder than the benchmark, with the seriousness being a little less than you would normally associate with a 5a route. Thus you would expect the climb to be quite tricky but with good protection. Conversely, a VS 4b route would have no very hard moves, but the seriousness would be as for a route that was trickier. The climb, therefore, would not be too difficult to ascend, but may not have as much protection as you would normally expect at that grade.

'Pink wall', VS 5a,
Pass of Ballater – steep
but well protected

WHERE TO START?

As already mentioned, you will probably only start to get an idea of how the grading system works after climbing a few routes. You may find the following useful to get you up and running.

- **Easy** The UK grading system starts here. This level of climb will be one with a great number of large holds, quite possibly set back at an amenable angle. It will present little difficulty to anyone keen to get on with climbing, but will still present the possibility of a fall, so ropework and gear placement skills will be paramount. My daughter seconded her first proper rock climb at the grade of 'Easy' when she was four years old. However, that is not to say that the grade is a doddle, and great care should be exercised at all times.

- **Moderate** This is the next grade up, and will be a little trickier. It should present few problems to a keen and sensible group, but may be quite steep, albeit on large holds. A number of classic mountain routes will be at this grade.

- **Diff and V. Diff** The top grades that most people getting into climbing will want to try. They cover a variety of route types – chimneys, slabs, corners and so on – with the route being a bit steeper than for the last two grades, and the holds requiring a little more thought prior to being used.

To recap, I suggest that you start out with the lowest possible grade of climb and see how that feels. You can easily work your way up on to harder levels. It's best to start with something too easy than too hard. If you have a bad experience early on you could be put off climbing altogether.

Getting to the route can be more exciting than the actual climbing!

2 EQUIPMENT

Note

A helmet will not only save you from debris or gear dropped from above, it will also protect your head in the event of a fall. In addition, if you are belaying, it will prevent you from banging your head if you are pulled forward when holding a leader fall. Although a lot of magazines show pictures of climbers without helmets, any type of head injury is extremely serious, and it is not worth taking a chance with your life.

If you have ever strolled through a climbing shop or looked at sites on the Internet, you will be aware that there is a huge array of tantalising climbing equipment available. The trick is to buy what will be appropriate for the type of climbing you wish to do and avoid the 'toys' – those fancy pieces of kit that look great but have no particular use at the crag.

There are important standards for climbing equipment manufacture. The UIAA (Union Internationale des Associations d'Alpinisme) has had a very sound voluntary code of practice in place for a number of years, and gear meeting their test criteria will bear a UIAA stamp. However, the PPE (Personal Protective Equipment) standards have been a legal requirement for a number of years in Europe. Equipment that satisfies this standard will be marketed with a CE (Conformité Européene) symbol. This shows that it conforms to the relevant sections of the European legislation as far as manufacturing requirements are concerned, and indicates that it can legally be sold in the European member countries.

I have listed below some items of the most important kit, and given a few pointers as to what may be appropriate where. There will inevitably be many factors to consider when buying kit, and your final choice will be largely down to personal preference.

Helmet

Modern helmets are lightweight and strong

This is an essential piece of gear, and should be one of your first purchases. Gone are the days when helmets looked like (and weighed the same as) coal scuttles. Modern helmets are lightweight, strong and comfortable. Take a hat with you when buying a helmet to make sure that it can be adjusted sufficiently to accommodate your hat underneath it during the colder months.

Harness

There are many different types of harness available, and the final decision will often come down simply to how comfortable it feels when being worn. There are a few other points worth taking into account.

Firstly, if the harness is just going to be used for rock climbing you may decide to go for non-adjustable leg loops. This will make the harness a little lighter and less elaborate, but will preclude it from being worn if you are wearing bulky clothing, as in the winter or when a cold wind is blowing. If you want an all-round harness, suitable for rock climbing all year, go for adjustable leg loops.

Good, all-round harness

One of the most important sections will be the abseil loop, the sewn loop at the front that serves as a strong point. I wouldn't think about buying a harness without one of these as it has so many uses. The gear-racking layout is also important, as you need to have plenty of space for equipment. I prefer to have my gear loops forwards, with two on each side, so that I can get to everything easily. Padding aids comfort, although too much tends to get in the way and can also make the harness a bit sweaty in hot weather.

Rock boots

There are probably as many types of rock boot as there are harness! As these will be worn for long periods comfort is an important issue. My advice would be not to go for the eye-wateringly tight fit that some shops will try to persuade you to buy, but for something that feels quite snug. If your boots feel firm in the shop without socks they are probably the right size, as they will stretch up to half a size after some use. Really tight boots are the preserve of those climbing at the very top levels; you can always graduate to a pair of these after a while, once you have decided which direction your climbing career is going to take.

Rock boots often come with a choice of fastenings, either laces or Velcro. The lacing system will be better at this stage, as Velcro tends to be used on very technical boots where the fit is skin-tight, meaning that little adjustment is possible.

The information at the end of a climbing rope will tell you if it is the right one for you

Rope

Ropes come in a bewildering array of sizes and colours, and everyone you talk to will have their own view as to what type will be best for you to begin with. As a starting-out rope I would suggest that 50m of 10.5mm with a dry treatment would be a good all-rounder. A 60m rope would be more appropriate for climbing multi-pitch routes, but even here a 50m rope will be adequate. It needs to be designated as a 'full-weight' rope, denoted by a '1' in a circle on the tape around the end, and also on the packaging. Thinner ropes are designated as 'half ropes', denoted by a '½' in the circle. These must be used alongside another rope to give full strength, using techniques known as double- or twin-roping. This book covers predominantly single-rope climbing skills, and so a full-weight rope will fulfil your needs for now.

Carrying a rope

This is best done by 'flaking'. Flaking stops the rope from twisting and kinking, which does tend to happen if a rope is 'coiled' in the old-fashioned manner. It also enables you to carry the rope on your back, in much the same manner as a

(Top left) **STEP 1**
Starting flaking the rope by laying lap coils across your hand
(Top right) **STEP 2**
Wrap a few turns of rope around the coils
(Bottom left) **STEP 3**
Pull a loop through the top and place this over all the coils, pulling the ends tight
(Bottom right) **STEP 4**
The completed flaked rope will not kink or knot when uncoiled

MY INTRODUCTION TO
SEA-CLIFF CLIMBING

Growing up in the south of England, Swanage was my local crag and this is where I started my climbing career. For my first ever trip there I was accompanied by a crisp copy of Pete Crew's *Dorset* guidebook, a mate from school, a few sandwiches – and my mother's old washing line. I was particularly proud of the latter: it *looked* like a climbing rope (albeit a tad on the short and thin side) and was nicely coiled, just as I'd seen on TV. (You can probably tell by now that we had no idea what we were about to get in to; even the legend on the inside cover of the guide that stated 'the pages in this book will easily separate after a thorough wetting' didn't stand out as sufficient warning.)

Suffice to say that we were lucky to get away with our lives. Heading straight for the Cattle Troughs area we avoided the many sections of cliff that would have entailed an abseil to reach the start of the climbs. With our meagre knowledge and equipment that would almost certainly have proved fatal. As it was, I'm sure that only youthful ignorance and stubbornness kept us alive that day, along with the fact that we didn't fall off anything and so test the recently liberated washing line. We were both soaked from the waves crashing onto the ledges at the base of the routes, and retired stunned, numb – and not a little frightened – after a few hours to the safety of the bus back home.

Sea cliffs, I quickly learned, are unforgiving places. You need to not only be able to abseil in, but more importantly be able to climb back out again. You need to know about tide times, the state of the sea, how to belay at the bottom as well as at the top, and have some mechanism in place for getting help if you do not return home at a given time.

Sea cliffs are also stunning places: wonderful solitude, the rock under your fingertips vibrating with every crash of the waves, the bright sunshine glinting off the sea and a slight breeze cooling you in the summer sun. This is why, despite my initial experience, sea-cliff climbing became a very important part of my life in the vertical, and I still look forward to trips to the coast with great anticipation.

Mind you – I quickly learnt a lot more about it after that first trip. I even went out and bought myself a rope.

Note

Take good care of your rope as this will extend its life. Carefully read and follow the instructions that are attached to it when bought, as these will outline cleaning procedures and give details about its lifespan, as well as other useful information. Make sure that you don't tread on your rope, as this can cause grit to enter the weave and cause damage. Store it dry and loosely flaked in a cool, dark place, and never use it for anything other than climbing. When flaking it, feel along the length of the rope for any flat spots or inconsistencies in the weave, and if you are ever in any doubt about its ability to perform well, have it checked professionally or simply discard it and buy a replacement.

2

EQUIPMENT

rucksack, when walking down from the top of the crag or when abseiling.

A rope carried in this way will be easy to undo when needed. Simply lift off the final loop and unwrap the coils. You can now place the whole rope on the ground and run it through hand over hand to check it for knots. If it has been flaked correctly the only thing you may find is a loop through a loop, which is easily remedied.

To carry the rope on your back, leave a couple of metres of tail. Put the rope behind you and bring the ends forward over your shoulders, around your back (over the flaked rope to keep it from swinging about) and then round to the front again. Tie the ends together with a reef knot.

A flaked rope tied to the climber's back is easy to carry

Snapgate karabiners

These are used when leading to allow quick clipping of any gear being placed for protection. There are various shapes and sizes, but they can be put into two main categories: those with **solid gates** and those with **wire gates**.

The advantage of a wire gate is threefold.

- They weigh less than an equivalent-size solid gate.
- The gate closure is performed by the clever positioning of the wire gate; there are no moving parts which could break or jam (unlike the solid gate, which often has a spring incorporated into its design).
- Most important is the mass of the gate. When a fall occurs, the passage of the rope through a karabiner sets up vibration. This can be sufficient to open and close a solid gate very quickly. If the point of loading on the karabiner – the stage at which the fall stops – coincides with the gate being open, this massively reduces its strength. A wire gate, as it has less mass, is less affected by the vibration and thus unlikely to be in the open position when the rope tightens after a fall.

Solid gate *(left)* **and wire gate** *(right)* **snap karabiners**

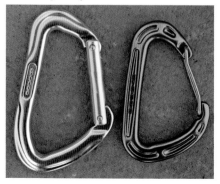

Although I prefer wire gates there is nothing to stop you using solid gate karabiners for your rack of gear (see page 31), but I would recommend supplementing them with wire gates over time.

Snapgate karabiners have either straight or bent gates. A bent gate allows easier clipping of the rope – especially when making 'desperate' clips – but there is also a slight increase in the chance of the rope unclipping during a fall in some situations, particularly if the gear has been clipped incorrectly (see Chapter 9).

It is also essential that a bent gate karabiner is always used at the rope end of any protection and never clipped into the gear itself; any twisting motion could cause it to come undone in extreme circumstances.

Straight *(left)* **and bent gate** *(right)* **snap karabiners**

2

EQUIPMENT

Screwgate karabiners

These have a sleeve on the gate that is fastened to prevent accidental opening. This is important when they are used as part of an anchor system, or when connecting a belay or abseil device to a climber. They are often categorized into two types: D-shape and 'HMS' or 'pear-shape'. The contrast is obvious from the photograph below.

It is important to know how the two differ under use.

- The strongest axis of a karabiner is along the back bar, and the **D-shape** will automatically align the rope in the correct position. This makes it the stronger of the two overall (although this will not matter too much in careful everyday use).
- The **HMS** does not have a tight bend at the end of the back bar, thus any load could fall some distance from it, so making the karabiner weaker than the 'D'.
- However, the **HMS** is great for clipping big knots or gear into, and will work well with a variety of belay and abseil devices. Its big advantage is when using an Italian hitch, as it allows the knot to work in the correct manner (since it is not forced into a tight corner). This function will become more obvious once we look at alternative belay methods (see Chapter 8).

'D'-shape *(left)* **and HMS** *(right)* **karabiners**

There are also different methods of locking mechanism. Many karabiners will use a sleeve that you need to tighten manually (don't overdo it: make it snug then turn it back a little, otherwise it could jam), while others

Close-up of a 'ball-lock'
karabiner, where the green
button has to be depressed
and the sleeve rotated
in order to open the gate

have an automatic facility. Automatic locking karabiners have a one- or two-stage function:

- **Single-stage** You just rotate or pull down on the sleeve, depending upon the design, and the gate can be swung open.
- **Two-stage** Either rotate the sleeve then pull it back, or press a button and then rotate.

I rarely use self-locking karabiners, but always go for the two-stage system as this seems to be safer than the single-stage operation.

Extenders

Sometimes known as 'quick-draws' or 'tie-offs', these are an essential part of a leader's rack. They consist of a short length of sling with a snapgate karabiner at each end. Once a piece of gear has been placed, one karabiner is clipped into it and the other karabiner is used to hold the rope. For most styles of climbing a selection of different-length extenders can be carried, from around 15–30cm. This enables runners off to the side of the climbing line to be used effectively.

Types of extender

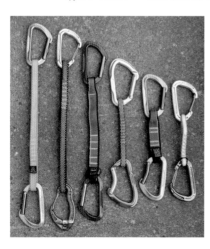

Extenders can be bought ready set-up with karabiners, or you can buy the sewn tape loops and add your own karabiners – buying ready-made sets will often work out cheaper. The sewn loops are either open like mini-slings, or have the middle parts attached so that the karabiners sit in their own loops on the ends. Make sure that neither of the karabiners is held too tightly by the stitching or by any rubber keeper device, as this will affect how they react when moved by the rope. If there is a separate keeper remove it to allow the karabiner to hang freely.

Slings

Slings are available in a number of lengths and widths, but the following are particularly useful (note that sewn slings are generally sold in flat measured lengths in centimetres, but are still often referred to by circumference in feet).

- **4ft (60cm) sling** made from a narrow fabric such as Dyneema. This length is very useful when equipped with two snapgate karabiners as it can be used as a long extender for off-line runners. The narrow fabric makes it easy to handle.
- **8ft (120cm) sling** made from a wider tape is extremely useful, and should be equipped with a screwgate karabiner. It can be used as an anchor or a running belay and, being made from thicker tape than the 4ft sling, is a little more robust.
- **16ft (240cm) sling** is the 'Big Daddy' and has many uses. For general outcrop use a wide fabric will be hard-wearing, but if you are going to venture on to multi-pitch routes you may wish to go for the thinner Dyneema, as this makes the sling very easy to handle when tying into anchor points. This sling should also be furnished with a screwgate karabiner.

Carrying slings is sometimes a problem, although with a bit of thought can be made quite easy. The short slings can be carried on your harness doubled through each other (see below). The medium-sized sling can be doubled, taken

(Below left) **Short slings with two karabiners on being doubled. They can then be carried like extenders.**
(Below right) **Carrying an 8ft (120cm) sling**

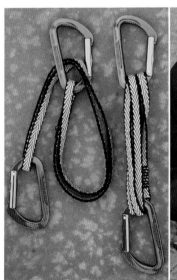

over the shoulder, then under one arm and clipped into itself. This enables you to take it off with one hand (not possible if you wrap it over your head). When carrying the long sling, double it and clip it into itself, then take it over your shoulder and under the other arm.

Belay device

This crucial piece of kit has a number of jobs, such as belaying a leader, belaying a second, and also doubles up as an abseil device.

There are two main categories:

- **Passive** where you control all the braking of a fall.
- **Active** where the device itself – although not hands-off – helps you by locking off, either through rotation or by internal moving parts (akin to a car seatbelt). A passive device is ideal for the techniques covered in this book.

Belay devices can be split further into different categories, the main two being:

- **Slick** which has a large aperture through which the rope fits. If the rope is thin – say less than 10.2mm – it may have difficulty holding it in the event of a fall.
- **Grabbing** devices often allow more control on thinner ropes (and sometimes too much on thick ropes, especially if abseiling), either on account of their shape or by the use of a channel through which the held rope is run. This channel will usually have a ribbed surface, providing extra friction that makes controlling the rope easier.

Variety of belay devices

Devices will normally have two slots to accommodate two ropes at the same time, useful for both double- or twin-rope techniques. This is also an important feature for abseiling, which is often done using two lengths of the same rope at once.

Wires

This is a generic name given to wedges of metal attached to the end of a swaged wire loop, often simply referred to as 'nuts' (the use of these and other equipment for protection is covered in detail in Chapter 7). They are, in fact, very technical pieces of kit and have been designed to exacting standards and great tolerances, and are the basic protection equipment for most climbers. The heads measure from a couple of millimetres to a couple of centimetres across, and the strength varies from 2kN (see Appendix 1) on the smallest to 12kN on

Set of wires

the larger sizes. Most climbers will carry a rack of wires made up of two sets of 1–10, all doubled up, although the final make-up will be down to personal preference. These will often be carried on the harness on two karabiners; I tend to have sizes 1–6 on one krab and 7–10 on the other. This means that you have a range of sizes to hand, useful once you have learnt to recognise which one fits which crack. Many wires are colour-coded for ease of identification.

You may see very tiny wires called 'micro-wires' for sale, as well as some others with very irregularly shaped heads. These are intended for a specific purpose, often for a one-off placement on a particular route. It is best – at least in the early stages of your climbing career – to stick to regular concave/convex designs.

Camming devices

These are often known as 'SLCD's (spring-loaded camming devices) – see Chapter 7. Most climbers will refer to them by the trade name – such as Friends or Quadcams – but camming devices or cams is generic enough for us. They are an extremely useful, albeit expensive, piece of kit. You don't need to buy them when setting up a basic rack, but once you get hold of one and try it out you won't know how you survived before!

The smallest cam/crack size is about 12mm, and the largest weighs in at a whopping 140mm (even bigger ones are available for specialist purposes). Two main considerations that will affect your choice:

- Firstly, they come in **rigid-stem** and **flexible-stem** versions. The rigid stem gives a good solid placement, but many climbers will now opt for the flexible-stem version as it is more forgiving when placed in a horizontal crack and fallen on – some rigid stems, especially older designs, could bend or even snap.
- Secondly is the decision of whether to go for **three-** or **four-cam** units. Three-cam units are generally narrower across the width of the cams, so are useful in the smaller sizes. Four-cam units are very stable, so are well suited to bigger sizes that will be used in wider cracks. It is unusual to find a three-cam unit on anything bigger than a size 2, so most people go for four cams.

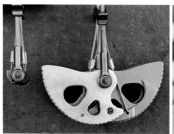

(Above right)
Four- and a three-cam unit

(Above left)
Size 0 and size 4 cam

Some designs incorporate a sewn sling that can be extended. This can help to avoid rope drag around bulges or if the placement is a little way off-line.

(Right)
Cam sling at normal length

(Far right)
Cam sling extended

Rockcentrics

These are basically a large version of a wire – but without the wire! Also referred to as chocks (and a reworking of the original 'Hexentrics' – still favourite with many people), the Rockcentric is available in large sizes and nicely complements our rack of wires.

However, they are a slightly different shape and work well in a variety of placements.

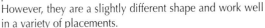

(Above) **Rockcentrics**
(Below) **Nut key**

They are frequently supplied with the tape or rope already stitched or tied in place. It is possible to buy them loose and tie them yourself, but in this case make sure you are using the correct material for the job. For instance, tying Spectra or Dyneema tape will not work as the fibres are quite slippery, and the resulting piece of gear will be very dangerous. Check with the supplier of the rope or tape you intend to use to thread the chocks to ensure that it is up to the job, also as to the best knot to use.

Rockcentrics work by a basic camming action, with the pull on the affixed tape making them jam tighter in a crack. If we have a rack of wires up to number 10, I would choose to start my Rockcentric sizing from there and go up for perhaps four sizes. You would end up with quite a large piece of gear, handy for a variety of situations and placements.

Nut key

This will be the best money you'll ever spend! A nut key is an invaluable tool for a second to carry in order to remove wires and other gear that has become jammed in place. Normally consisting of a long flat bar with a hook at one end, a key will very soon pay for itself (and may even get you some free gear by allowing you to winkle out someone else's kit!).

Chalk bag

This is included here only for completeness, and hopefully you won't be rushing out to buy one. Chalk is useful where the climbing is hard and fingers get sweaty, such as when training on an indoor climbing wall. Outside, however – unless the route is quite hard – the use of chalk should be discouraged. Chalk is slightly abrasive, which is how it aids finger friction. If used on the holds of an easy route, the hands and feet of subsequent climbers will have the effect of polishing the hold: the chalk particles work as a scourer. As more people will tend to climb easier graded routes than

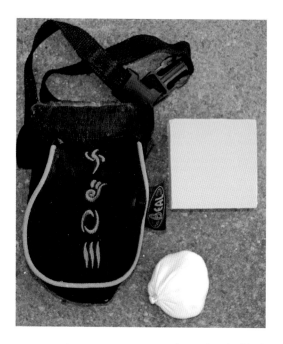

hard ones, and if many of them use chalk, the rock will very quickly become polished and slippery. Only use chalk on a hard route, when you are bouldering or climbing indoors.

Prusik loops

A prusik loop is a very useful piece of kit, with two being carried for more advanced techniques. It is commonly used for protecting an abseil, and can also be used in a simple hauling system to get your partner over a hard section of the climb. The loop is made up from just over 1m of 6mm accessory cord, purchased direct from the reel in a climbing shop. It is tied together with a double fisherman's knot, and should measure about 40cm long from end to end when laid flat.

Chalk bag, with ball and block chalk

Note

These days all technical equipment is manufactured and sold to rigorous standards. However, there is some cheap gear on the market (although not normally in reputable shops) which has been made in Eastern Europe and the Far East. This kit will often not have gone through the same processes and testing as stamped gear, and should be treated with extreme caution – or rejected altogether.

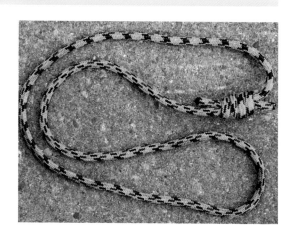

Prusik loop, tied with a double fisherman's knot

GEAR RACK

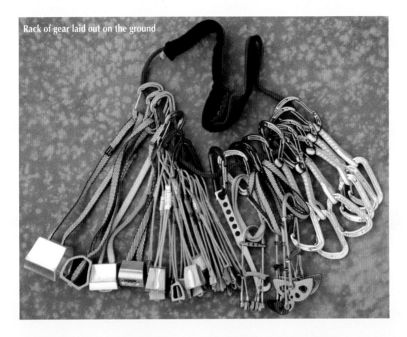

Rack of gear laid out on the ground

I have outlined a list of kit below that would be a really good rack for starting out. As far as possible I have put them in the order in which they should be purchased: buying a rope will probably be more important than getting hold of a couple of prusik loops, for example. This gear list will be ideal for routes up to VS (and probably higher).

Bear in mind that some rock types will predispose themselves to accepting different types of gear. For instance, if you are climbing on sandstone regularly you may wish to increase the number of camming devices. Conversely if you are climbing on limestone a good range of wires will possibly be of more use.

- Harness
- Helmet
- Rock boots
- Belay device
- Rope (50m x 10.5mm)
- HMS screwgate karabiners x 3
- 4ft (60cm) sling x 2
- 8ft (120cm) sling x 2
- 16ft (240cm) sling x 1
- D-shape screwgates x 3
- Curved wires 1–10 x 2 sets
- Rockcentrics 6, 7, 8, 9

- Nut key and small carrying karabiner x 1
- Camming devices, flexible stem, 1, 2, 3
- Extenders x 6
- Snapgate karabiners: 2 for carrying wires, 4 for carrying hex's, 12 for extenders, 4 for 4ft (60cm) slings, 3 for camming devices. Total = 25
- Prusik loops x 2
- Chalk bag

3 KNOTS

If there is one subject that is likely to send shivers down the spine of anyone starting out in climbing, this is it! There is a plethora of books available extolling the virtues of this one or that, often resulting in general confusion. Luckily you only need to learn a few in order to get started, and you could even get away with just a figure of eight (in all its forms) and a clove hitch. The following knots, however, are worth learning.

Figure of eight rewoven

This very important knot is the standard way of attaching yourself to your harness. It looks like an '8' and so is easily recognised on both you and your partner. It should be tied so that the loop created is no bigger than the abseil loop on the front of your harness; if any larger it will be awkward to use when belaying and tying onto anchors. Once the knot is

FIGURE OF EIGHT REWOVEN

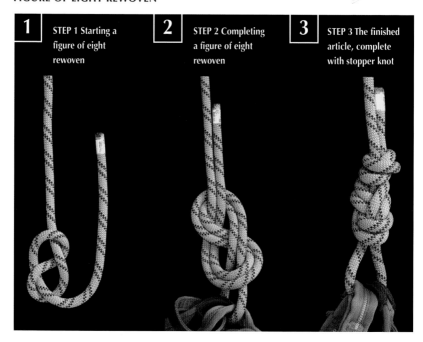

1 STEP 1 Starting a figure of eight rewoven

2 STEP 2 Completing a figure of eight rewoven

3 STEP 3 The finished article, complete with stopper knot

tied it should be finished off with half a double fisherman's (see below) as a stopper knot, pushed up snug to the eight. The resulting tail should be no more than 3–10cm long.

Figure of eight on a bight
This variation of the figure of eight is very useful for attaching yourself to a belay anchor. It ends up looking just like the figure of eight on your harness, but is tied in a slightly different manner. It has the advantage of being quick to tie, does not require the use of any gear (such as a karabiner), and will tighten during loading, an important property when trying to reduce the loading at the anchor.

Another variation of this knot can be tied into the end of the rope. This is most likely to be used when clipping into the end, rather than tying in, when bottom- or top-roping (although many will still prefer to tie in for security). As with the original, it should be finished off with half a double fisherman's as a stopper knot.

(Above left) **Figure of eight on a bight**

(Above right) **Figure of eight on the bight on the end of the rope**

Double bowline
Some people prefer to use this knot for tying into the harness, as it can be undone easily after loading. However,

DOUBLE BOWLINE

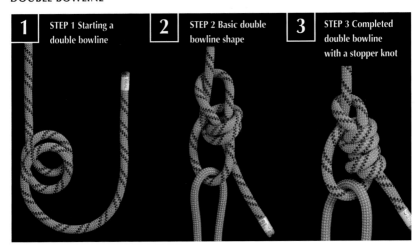

1 STEP 1 Starting a double bowline

2 STEP 2 Basic double bowline shape

3 STEP 3 Completed double bowline with a stopper knot

most climbers still like to tie on using the figure of eight rewoven as it is instantly recognisable, and it is possible to tie the bowline incorrectly.

It is essential that half a double fisherman's is tied as a stopper knot, butted snugly up against the main knot, otherwise the bowline could undo in some situations. One of its main uses is to tie an abseil rope to an anchor, as it can be loaded repeatedly but then undone quite easily at the end of the day.

Italian hitch

This very handy knot – also known as the 'Munter' hitch – can be used for both belaying and abseiling. It can be utilised in a variety of roles as a belaying knot, not least when you have accidentally dropped your belay device down the crag and are left holding just the karabiner! For

ITALIAN HITCH

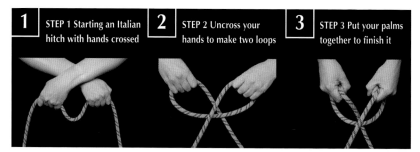

1 STEP 1 Starting an Italian hitch with hands crossed

2 STEP 2 Uncross your hands to make two loops

3 STEP 3 Put your palms together to finish it

Note

It is very important that the Italian hitch is clipped into an HMS karabiner and not a D-shape one. The hitch needs to rotate easily around the end of the karabiner, an important property when belaying as the rope may be taken in and paid out and the hitch will need to swivel freely. If a D-shape is used the hitch could get jammed at the tight bend at the end of the back bar.

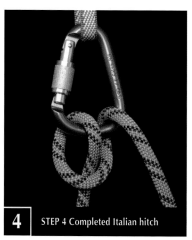

4 STEP 4 Completed Italian hitch

abseiling, we could put forward a similar scenario. It does tend to twist the rope after a lot of use, but this can be solved by simply shaking the rope out and unwrapping any kinks.

Clove hitch

This is an important knot, and very valuable when used to secure yourself to an anchor when belaying. It is quick to tie, easily adjustable and locks off when loaded. It is best if the clove hitch is clipped into an HMS karabiner, as this will allow it to sit in the correct fashion, whereas a D-shape may cause it to ride up over itself. If you do have to use a D-shape check that the knot is sitting correctly.

CLOVE HITCH

1 STEP 1 Starting a clove hitch with hands crossed

2 STEP 2 Uncross your hands

3 STEP 3 Place one hand behind the other

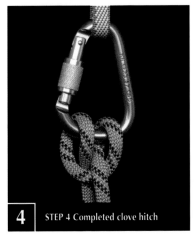

4 STEP 4 Completed clove hitch

Note

Make sure that you cross your hands in the correct manner, otherwise you will end up with just a couple of loose loops and not a clove hitch. With a little practice, you will be able to tie this knot quickly and without thinking about it too hard.

French prusik

Tied with a prusik loop, this is a very useful little knot, particularly as it can be used as a safety back-up when abseiling. It slides up and down the rope, but will tighten and grip it when loaded. Additionally, it can be released when under load, such as when you wish to continue abseiling after a halt, perhaps to retrieve some stuck gear from the crag.

Keep the double fisherman's knot, tied to create the loop, out of the way whilst you wrap it around the climbing

French prusik. Keep the wraps neat around the main rope.

rope several times. How many wraps depends on many factors: you may be abseiling on two ropes (or just one doubled up), the rope may be wet or dry, shiny or a bit rough, and all these will make a difference of a wrap or two. Once around the rope, the two ends of the prusik loop are clipped together with a screwgate karabiner that is in turn clipped to the appropriate strong point. Loading the system causes the wrappings to tighten around the main rope, thus gripping it. To release the prusik, pull down on the top of it with your fingertips, along the line of the main rope.

Note

It is very important that the French prusik is never used in a situation where it can be shock-loaded. If this happens there is a chance that the loop will slip down the main rope, either stripping it of its outer sheath or, if the slide is of some distance, the prusik loop itself may generate enough heat to melt through.

Double fisherman's knot

This is a handy 'workhorse' of a knot, used to join two sections of rope together, such as when constructing a prusik loop, when joining ropes for abseiling or, very often, when half a double fisherman's is used as a stopper knot to back up a figure of eight or bowline. Take a little time to make sure that the knot is tied neatly and looks symmetrical once completed.

DOUBLE FISHERMAN'S KNOT

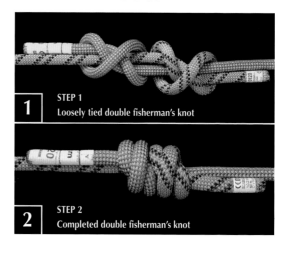

1 STEP 1
Loosely tied double fisherman's knot

2 STEP 2
Completed double fisherman's knot

Overhand knot

This mainly functions as an isolation knot when using a sling to equalise an anchor. It is very simple to tie, although with very thin slings you may prefer to opt for a figure of eight. It can be quite difficult to undo, especially when tied in thin Spectra or Dyneema slings, so a figure of eight may be chosen instead. It is also used as a knot for joining abseil ropes (see Chapter 11), where it is essential that a figure of eight is not used.

Lark's-foot

This knot is sometimes used to attach a sling to an anchor. However, it is quite a weak method and there are better options available, such as simply clipping the ends of the sling together with a karabiner. A lark's-foot is suitable when attaching a cow's-tail to your harness when abseiling in a multi-pitch situation. It can be used to join two slings together if you are running out of karabiners, but make sure that the resulting knot is neat and looks like a reef knot (see below).

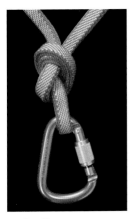

Overhand knot

(Above left) A sling lark's-footed around an anchor, not a very strong way to belay and not recommended

(Left) Joining two slings with a double lark's-foot

Reef knot

This is a useful knot for a couple of reasons. Firstly, it is handy if you are wrapping the flaked rope behind you in order to carry it like a rucksack, as it is a good way to tie the ends off in front of you. Secondly, it is a handy knot to use inside a double fisherman's when joining two abseil ropes together, as it stops the knots from jamming together and becoming difficult to untie. If you remember the phrase 'right over left, left over right' you will end up with the correct knot each time. The 'left' and 'right' relate to the tails of the rope.

Reef knot

'Éclair de lune', 5+, Gorbio, Maritime Alps

4 TYING ON

In this section we will look at a number of basic yet essential skills which must be mastered before attempting to climb.

- How to tie onto the end of the rope, obviously important for both the leader and second.
- Different ways of tying onto one or more anchors.
- How to use a sling to bring two or three anchors down to one point, often useful in a multi-pitch climbing situation, or when fixing up a system such as a bottom rope (see Chapters 12 and 13).

TYING ONTO YOUR HARNESS

Being able to tie onto your harness effectively and securely is pivotal to being safe whilst climbing. It is amazing how often you see people on the crags with sloppy knots or tied onto the wrong point and so incorrectly connected to what is, in every sense of the word, their safety line.

Usually, you and your partner will need to be tied onto your harnesses. This not only gives a very strong attachment to the rope, it also provides a point from which the belay device can be operated, and a position to which any anchor ropes can be connected. The figure of eight rewoven will be the usual choice (although the bowline can also

Note

Don't let anyone disturb you for the few seconds it takes to tie onto the end of the rope, whether you are leading, seconding, top- or bottom-roping (see Chapters 9, 10 and 13). Being passed a piece of gear, for example, is distracting; it's easy to forget to finish the knot properly and to leave it half-tied. If someone calls you or hands you some gear when tying in, tell them to wait for a moment and complete the job properly.

A WORD OF WARNING

Clipping into the abseil loop with a karabiner will work if you are going to be top- or bottom-roping over a short distance, but it should *never* be used as a method of attachment to the rope when leading. If a fall occurred and the karabiner slipped sideways, the rope could run over the gate at the point of loading, greatly reducing the karabiner's strength. If you do choose to clip into the rope with a screwgate for top- or bottom-roping, some manufacturers sensibly recommend two screwgate karabiners are used, clipped so that the gates open in opposition to each other. A figure of eight knot on the end of the rope would be the best one to use.

be used). The only drawback of the latter is that the stopper knot is on the inside radius of the loop created by tying in, and can get in the way of subsequent connections.

It is important that the correct section of the harness is threaded, normally the same line as taken by the abseil loop. Some harness designs – particularly those made for group use – have a single flat-loop attachment point, and the rope will be tied around this. Check in the instruction booklet that came with your harness to ensure that you are threading the rope around the correct sections.

Once tied, the resulting loop should be no bigger than the abseil loop, or a little smaller than fist size. Any larger and subsequent attachments will be awkward to complete and there may be problems with belaying. Any smaller and there won't be enough room for any subsequent connections to be tied on or clipped in.

(Above left) **Clipped onto the rope using two screwgates back to back.** *Do not* **use this method of attachment for leading routes.**

(Above right) **Tied on with a figure of eight rewoven and half a double fisherman's stopper knot**

TYING ONTO ANCHORS WITH THE ROPE

There are a number of methods of securing the belayer to one or more anchors. Not understanding how this process works – and how vital it is – risks putting the climber in real danger. Efficiently tying onto an anchor is relevant whether belaying from the top or the bottom of a cliff, and the process for both is the same.

To get to this point, make sure you know how to tie a clove hitch and a figure of eight on the bight. Remember that a clove hitch is only of use if you can reach the karabiner into which it is clipped. If the anchor karabiner is much more than an arm's length away it's better to use a figure of eight on the bight.

Tip

....

The figure of eight on a bight is an excellent knot once it has been mastered. Although the knot is not difficult to tie, you may find getting the tension right between you and the anchor tricky at first. Have a practice at home, in order to save time on the crag. Select a good anchor (something that won't be destroyed if you pull on it!), such as a stairpost, then sit at a certain point and get the tension right after the knot is tied. Having an anchor at the top of the stairs, and sitting two steps from the bottom, provides a very realistic rehearsal of the anchoring method.

(Below left) **A clove hitch tying-on system**
(Below right) **Tying on with a figure of eight on the bight**

One anchor point within reach

As the screwgate karabiner to which you will be attaching yourself is easily within reach, you can clip into this with a clove hitch. The clove hitch is very adjustable, but will lock off under load.

1 The hitch is tied onto the rope coming from the tie-in point on your harness.
2 Clip it in and then adjust it so that the rope between you and the anchor is tight.
3 Make sure that you end up seated not too close to the edge of the cliff but where you can see and communicate with your climbing partner effectively.

One anchor point out of reach

As already mentioned, only use a clove hitch if you can reach the karabiner into which it is to be clipped. As this anchor will be some distance away from you, a figure of eight on the bight will be better for attachment.

1 Clip the rope from your harness through the screwgate on the anchor, then get yourself into a suitable position at the top of the climb.
2 The figure of eight is now tied around the rope loop created by tying onto your harness at the start of the climb.
3 Ensure that you are tight on the anchor once the knot has been completed. This will be tricky to manage the first few times, so a bit of prior practice will pay dividends.
4 Remember that the loop end left after tying the knot should be around 60cm long.

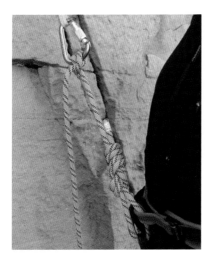

5 Once it has been tied, pull all four bits of rope that comprise the knot to tighten it.

Two anchor points within reach
1 Take the rope from your harness, tie a clove hitch and clip it into the first anchor.
2 Leave a little slack rope, and put a clove hitch onto the second anchor.
3 The rope is now brought back to your harness and tied on with a figure of eight on the bight. By doing this you ensure that the load is shared equally between the anchor points.
4 If once the figure of eight has been tied there is a little slack in the system, the clove hitches can be adjusted to get the tension right. There is also some leeway in shifting your belay position slightly, as one or both of the clove hitches can be adjusted in order to compensate for change in load.

Two anchor points out of reach
1 The rope is clipped into both anchor points. This means that it now runs from your harness and up to the first anchor, across to the second anchor and then back down the cliff.
2 Move to your belay position, making sure that you take the rope running between the two anchors with you. This will probably mean that you need to have a hand on the rope coming up and over the edge of the cliff, feeding it towards the anchor as you make your way backwards. This will help to reduce the friction in the system and make moving a little easier.

Tip
When tying onto the rope that runs over the edge of the cliff, pull up some slack and trap it gently under your foot. This makes it much easier to tie the knot, as you do not have to fight against the weight of the rope.

(Below left) **Tying on with two clove hitches**
(Below right) **Tying onto two anchors out of reach**

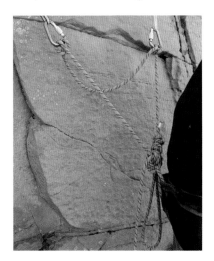

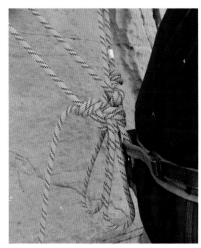

Note

Once you understand how to use a clove hitch and a figure of eight, you can attach yourself to almost any number and sequence of anchors, in reach, out of reach, and so on. The main limitations will be the availability of sensible anchors, the length of the rope – and the patience of your partner!

3   Once at your stance pull the rope coming out of the first anchor tight, and tie this onto yourself using a figure of eight on the bight.
4   Pull the rope from the second anchor tight and repeat the process of tying in with a figure of eight.
5   Once both knots are tied, ensure that the load is equally shared between both anchors. Again, prior practice will pay dividends.

One anchor point in reach, the other out of reach
1   From your harness, go to the furthest anchor, clip in and come back to your belay position, tying in with a figure of eight on the bight.
2   Use the rope coming out of the figure of eight and take it up to the nearer anchor, clipping in with a clove hitch and adjusting it as necessary.

Tying onto one anchor point out of reach – alternative method
1   Clip the rope into the screwgate karabiner and get into your belay position.
2   Have a second screwgate to hand, preferably an HMS, and clip this into the rope tie-in loop on your harness.
3   Tie a clove hitch in the rope and clip it into this karabiner. Even though the anchor is out of reach, you now have the ability to adjust the tension on the belay rope.

I would always plump for the figure of eight method instead, for the following reasons:

(Below left) **Using a system for one anchor in reach and another some distance away**
(Below right) **Using the clove hitch at the harness method**

- Firstly, there is now a screwgate karabiner on your tie-in loop, and it's good to keep any extra metalwork away from here to avoid it getting cluttered.

- Secondly, one of the main advantages of the figure of eight is that it has some shock-absorbing properties. In the event of a fall – and in particular where there is significant loading on the system such as created in a leader fall – the knot will tighten when loaded. This has the effect of reducing the shock-loading on the anchor system, which is important if the anchors aren't quite as good as they could be.

Note

If you do choose to use the clove hitch on the harness method, don't be tempted to place more than one clove hitch in the karabiner. The clove hitches will be extremely difficult to adjust, as they will butt up against each other making feeding the rope through very awkward. Also the load transmitted to the karabiner will then most likely be some distance from the back bar of the karabiner, which is the strongest line. Any significant loading will therefore exert a levering force on the gate section of the karabiner, which is to be avoided if at all possible. Simply tying in with two figure of eights will avoid these problems.

EQUALISING ANCHORS USING A SLING

Before attaching the rope it might be preferable to link two gear placements – such as a couple of wires – together. This method will often be used on a multi-pitch route, or where dealing with one anchor is more practical and quicker than using two. The situations where linking anchors using a sling are relevant are mentioned in Chapter 12.

There are a number of ways of bringing two anchor points down to one using a sling, but the following two are suitable for almost every situation where joining two anchors together is needed. The first one is the quickest and has the advantage of looking right once it's been done! The second is also fairly quick and has the advantage of using less sling length, helpful if the anchors are some distance apart.

Method 1

1   Make sure that each wire has a screwgate attached.
2   Clip the sling into each of these, and do the gates up.

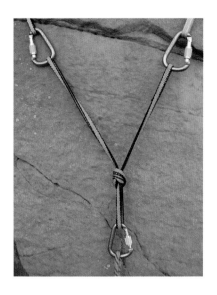

(Above left)
**Equalising anchors by using an
overhand knot around the sling**

(Above right)
**Equalising anchors by tying an
overhand knot to make two
individual loops in the sling**

3 Pulling the sling down from between the wires, tie an overhand or figure of eight knot around it.

4 This then has another screwgate karabiner clipped into it and will be the attachment point for your rope.

Method 2

1 Clip the sling into one of the karabiners and do the gate up.

2 Estimate where the attachment point will be (the position for the screwgate that will hold the rope) and tie an overhand knot loosely round the sling.

3 Now clip the other end into the second karabiner and do the gate up. By tying the overhand knot you have effectively divided the sling into two loops.

4 Clip the karabiner through which the rope is going to run into the first loop and then into the second. It will now sit on top of the overhand knot. If its position is not correct you can shuffle the overhand knot left or right a bit until you are satisfied that the load is shared equally.

5 Once you have done this, pull it snug. Take great care that you have clipped through each of the loops correctly and not just round the sling, as this will not hold the karabiner captive if one of the anchors pulls out.

5 CLIMBING CALLS

It is very important to learn and understand a series of climbing calls. These will be recognised just about wherever you go, and are used to clarify the situation between you and your second.

Obviously, if you are standing next to each other at the bottom of a route, or on a ledge on a multi-pitch climb, there is no need to go through a formal sequence. However, using a set series of instructions and statements will help prevent any misunderstanding when you are some distance apart. Bear in mind that distance, wind and other natural sounds such as a nearby river will all make communication difficult, so you need to be quite loud, clear and concise in your delivery.

The standard calls are as follows, and are listed in the order you might come across them during a leading session.

'Runner on'	From the leader when he has clipped into the first runner, so that the belayer knows that it's time to start paying attention. Until that time the belayer may have been 'spotting' the leader.
'Take in'	Meaning that the leader (but can also be used by the second later on) needs some slack rope to be taken in. This may be because he has come down a move or two or, in the case of a second, has climbed up a little out of sight of the belayer.
'Slack'	The rope is too tight and the leader (or possibly the second) needs a little more rope in order to move up or down.
'Watch me'	The climber, often the leader (but relevant to both leader and second) is about to make a tricky move and needs the confidence boost of knowing that the belayer is watching him closely, ready to hold a potential fall.
'Take'	Said just before either of the climbers falls off, or when one of them commits his weight to the rope in order to rest or remove gear.

As you can see, these calls cover a variety of situations and can be used whenever and wherever appropriate by any party member.

The next two are used between the leader and belayer once the leader is at the top of the climb or, in the case of a multi-pitch route, on an appropriate belay ledge.

'Safe'	Used by the leader once he is safe (a matter for some consideration – see below).
'You're off'	From the second, called once he has removed the leader's rope from his belay device.

Note

Calling 'safe' requires a great deal of thought. It might well be that on a pleasant day at a crag with a clean top you feel safe as soon as you have climbed over the edge and are standing upright. In other situations, on a grassy top-out in the drizzle with a breeze blowing, you probably won't be safe until you have connected yourself to the belay anchor system. Knowing when you are and are not safe is crucial, and I would urge you to err on the side of caution. If you are going to call safe as soon as you top-out, at least pull through a metre or two of rope before shouting. If your second doesn't hear you clearly and steps back to see what is going on, you won't be pulled over the cliff edge.

'Taking in'	From the leader once securely belayed, as he pulls up, hand over hand, the slack rope between him and the second.
'That's me'	From the second, when the rope comes snug onto his harness.
'Climb when you are ready'	From the leader, but only after he has put the rope through the belay device and checked that all screwgates are done up and that his ABC is correct (see Chapter 8).
'Climbing'	Called by the second, but he does not climb until he has heard the next call from the leader.
'OK'	The leader confirms that he has heard and is ready to belay.

This may seem to be a bit complicated, but you will soon get the idea and the sequence will become second nature after just a few routes.

To finish off, the following calls may be of use.

'Tight'	Most likely called by the second, or by anyone bottom-roping, normally just before he is about the fall off. The belayer puts his weight behind the rope, pulling it in tight through the belay device, which takes the stretch out of it, making the climber feel secure.
'Rope below'	A courtesy call, used when dropping or throwing the rope down the crag prior to abseiling. Always pause a moment before deploying it, and take a look down the crag if possible.
'Below'	The most feared of calls! This means that something has been dislodged, such as a stone or rock, and is falling towards anyone below. If you hear this call don't look up but keep your head tucked in. If you have knocked something off call out even if you don't think there is anyone else around, just in case.

5

CLIMBING CALLS

6 MOVING ON ROCK

The natural art of moving gracefully and effectively on rock is something we tend to lose the older we get. I remember being amazed at my daughters, aged three and four, moving fluently across easy ground and doing things quite naturally that climbing instructors spend a lot of time teaching adults. Layaways, mantelshelves and opposition holds all seemed to be second nature to them at that age, but I have noticed that as they get older they have to think more about how to move. Most of us, it seems, have natural ability; it just takes a bit of effort to refine it for climbing into adulthood.

This chapter covers a number of ways to use holds and to move across rock. The final choice will obviously be up to you and how you feel at any particular time, and you and your partner will probably use different approaches on the same piece of rock. You may not be the same height or weight, and will probably possess different strength ratios, all of which will affect the decision-making process.

TRAINING FOR CLIMBING

As this book covers the basics of rock climbing, giving you the technical skills to start leading on easy routes, I'm not going to go into detail about specific training regimes or fitness programmes. There is a wealth of information available for those who wish to get into a regular and specific climbing training programme. However, it is worth mentioning two very useful aids when learning to move across rock.

Bouldering

Many climbers see this as an activity in its own right, and will often boulder all day rather than set foot on a climb. It is an excellent way of training, as realistic as it can get, and dedicated boulderers are very strong and fit. However, we will treat bouldering as a means for learning how to use holds. All holds and movement techniques found on a climb can also be found on boulders, albeit after a little bit of searching. Crack lines allow you to practise finger and hand jamming, wider cracks allow for experimentation of layaway and layback techniques. All sorts of holds, such as

Bouldering is a good way of learning to use holds effectively

pockets, slopers and crimps can be found, and a little time spent trying them out can be very beneficial.

Climbing wall

There may be one near your home, and you might be a regular user already; if not a visit will be very worthwhile. Although far more clinical than bouldering, a climbing wall does have one distinct advantage – it's indoors! The wet and windy day when you wanted to go climbing need not be wasted after all, and a trip to the wall will not only give you exercise but will also provide a chance to try out a variety of moves in reasonable safety and comfort.

A climbing wall is a good place to practise if the weather is not conducive to training outdoors

Warming up

Warming-up is very important. During a bouldering or climbing wall session you will tend to climb a bit harder than when leading, and so the chance of injury is increased. There is a tendency to pull harder on smaller holds when the body is not ready, which can cause tendon or ligament damage. Warming up will help prepare our bodies and reduce the chance of injury. Try the following procedure:

- An activity that warms up your body, lasting for four or five minutes: jogging or running, or star jumps, anything that increases your heart rate and makes your lungs work hard to keep you supplied with oxygen. This increases blood flow to the muscle groups, preparing them for use.
- A short loosening up session should follow, flexing your joints to the full but without stretching them. Start with your toes and work your way up to your head, circling ankles and hips, swinging arms backwards and forwards, rotating wrists and wriggling fingers. This lubricates the joints, thus reducing injury potential.
- Stretching is important, and the following concentrates on the specific muscle groups involved in climbing. Make sure you are already warmed up before starting, or you could injure yourself. It is also important not to bounce or stretch so much that something hurts. Stand next to the wall or boulder, select a large hold and lean off to the left. Hold this for 15–20 seconds, then straighten up, swap hands and lean off to the right. Keep your feet on the ground so as to not over-stress the muscles. Now find a large hold above head height and repeat the sequence, leaning back on the hold. Find another hold and use both hands on it, feeling the stretch as you put a little weight on it. Use other holds, such as undercuts and finger pockets, to stretch specific areas. If you are going to have a big climbing session remember to stretch thighs and calves as well, as this will give you more flexibility and allow you to lift your feet higher without pulling a muscle. Leg stretching can be done on the floor, or using a suitable boulder or section of wall.
- Light bouldering or easy climbing on the wall should follow, concentrating on any body areas that still feel a little stiff. Keep it simple and slow at the start, building up after a while to whatever you wish to achieve for the session.

Performing a stretch, using a hold to help

Warming down

Warming down is also important, not least to prevent muscles from feeling sore the next day. Finish your session with

a little light bouldering or climbing, not with a 'last gasp' desperate series of moves. Rotating and flexing your joints for a couple of minutes will help to prevent any stiffness, and some light stretching of key areas will help with future flexibility and health. Of particular importance will be the forearms, wrists and fingers, as these will probably have taken the brunt of the work. Rotate and flex them for a while, then stretch them out lightly by leaning against a wall with your palms flat and fingers pointing downwards, moving your body position until the stretch is felt. You can also put your palms together in front of you, elbows out to the side, and push the heels of your hands lower whilst keeping your elbows in position. Remember to hold any stretch for at least 15–20 seconds, otherwise it will not be effective.

(Above left) **Stretching out wrists and forearms using a wall**

(Above right) **Pushing your palms together and down is also a very effective forearm stretch**

HANDHOLDS

There is a huge variety of holds available that can be gripped, jammed and pulled on, although most people usually end up using the same hold in a different manner.

One-finger pocket

This is one of the hardest holds as it requires great finger strength. Don't be tempted to try it out if you are not warmed up as a huge amount of pressure is placed on the finger joints. It is important to keep the other fingers very close to the one in the pocket, with the thumb wrapped over the top to give support and allow as little leverage as possible on the joints.

Using a one-finger pocket

Large pocket

This will allow more than one finger to be inserted, giving greater security. Any fingers that cannot fit in should be placed where they can give support, again with the thumb wrapped over the top if possible.

Small crimps

This is where a couple of fingertips can be placed on a small ledge. The finger joints are bent so that the hand looks as though it is gripping something, with the thumb being used across the top to keep them in place. This is a very tiring hold for any length of time, and practice is needed in order to feel comfortable and use it effectively.

Large crimps

(Top left) **Small crimp**
(Bottom left) **Large crimp being used with the thumb to one side**
(Bottom right) **A good jug**

These are fairly common on many rock types and, as they will most likely accommodate all four fingers, feel quite secure. Your thumb could go across the top to help keep the fingers in place, or could sit at the side with the fingers staying on the hold through their own strength.

Jugs

'Jug' is short for 'jug handle', implying that you can get your whole hand around the hold. It is used for any large hold (sometimes called 'thank God holds' as they often arrive just as you need them!). There is no particular technique for holding on, but it may be worth spending a moment swapping hands and resting. Some jugs will have space to accommodate both hands.

Pebbles

These are small intrusions that have eroded less than the surrounding rock surface. They protrude slightly and give the chance of a hold on an otherwise blank surface. As they very often are, quite literally, pebbles, they can be very smooth and difficult to grip and are often best 'pinched'.

Undercuts

These tend to be 'forgotten holds'; you often come across them only after searching for a while for a way past a particular problem. An undercut is surprisingly secure, despite having your hand upside down, usually below shoulder height, which means that your next hold cannot be particularly far above you. The best undercuts are upside-down jugs, and give a good and solid base from which to lean out and scan the route ahead.

(Top left) **Pinching a pebble**
(Top right) **Using an undercut hold**
(Bottom right) **Pinching a hold**

Pinches

These are good holds as long as your fingers can find a little purchase on the sides that they are gripping. Pinches that flare a little, so that your fingers can be held wider at the tips than at the base, are a little trickier to deal with and thus also rely a lot on friction. Wide pinches are very awkward indeed, requiring technique and strength to use them effectively.

Side pulls

These are very common on all types of rock, and often prove to be the answer to a successful move or key sequence. The use of a side pull will normally mean that

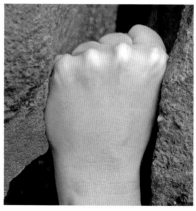

(Top left) **Using a side pull**
(Right) **Palming during**
a friction move
(Bottom left) **Fist jam**

you need to lean in the opposite direction and maintain this orientation until you are past the particular section. Side pulls tend to be like a vertical crimp, and treated in much the same way. However, as they are often used more for balance moves than purely pulling on they will tend to be less tiring.

Palming

This move is most frequently used on slab climbs, where the holds have run out and friction is the answer to moving on and up. In order to achieve maximum purchase your fingers, and thus palms, need to be facing downwards and the relevant arm straightened. This will allow your palm to keep in contact with the rock. The move is completed by pushing with your feet.

Fist jam

Jamming is definitely an acquired taste! It is sometimes not too comfortable but often very secure, and the only answer if an awkward crack is encountered. A fist jam relies mainly on the fact that the skeletal section of your hand is too big to pull through the width of the crack. It can be constructed with your hand either face on, with your palm facing away, or sideways on with your thumb on the outside. Placing your hand into the crack in the relevant orientation and then making a fist will produce a shape that is suitable for jamming.

Hand jam

This is slightly different to a fist jam as your hand will be open. Present your hand into the crack with all fingers straight, and then bring your thumb across your palm, arching your fingers at the same time. This has the effect of increasing the width at the base of the thumb, creating a section of flesh that will be able to jam into a suitably sized crack. This is a fairly common type of hand jam, and is very secure if the crack width is accommodating.

Finger jam

This is very useful for climbing thin cracks. Although it would not appear to be the most comfortable technique, it is good for negotiating sections of ground where other methods are proving ineffective, since it relies upon a jamming action and no particular strength. It is best used where the thumb is downwards. Having your hand with the thumb uppermost is quite possible but maybe not as secure.

(Below left) **Creating a hand jam by bringing the thumb across in front of the palm**
(Below right) **A finger jam with the thumb downwards**

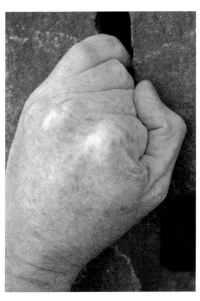

FOOTHOLDS

Smearing

When you use rock boots you will be aware that the soles are smooth, thus allowing maximum rubber-to-rock contact and consequently a lot of friction. Smearing is a technique where slabby climbs, in particular, are ascended by the use of friction alone.

The main contact area will be the front sole, and to stay on the rock you will need to keep your heel at around the same height as your toes, meaning that your foot is bent in a shallow 'U' shape. Press down with your toes to give the maximum possible purchase and to force the rubber onto the rock.

Although the rock may appear to be smooth all over, there will normally be a series of tiny bulges and surface imperfections that you can use to your advantage, giving you a bit more support and traction.

Edging

This is a very common technique where either the inner or outer edge of the boot is placed on an incut hold. This is usually done with the front part of the sole, with the heel and outer edge being lifted up from horizontal to help keep it in place.

Foot jamming

This is a useful way of ascending a cracked section of ground. Place your boot into the

(Top) **Smearing by keeping as much rubber as possible in contact with the rock**

(Middle) **Edging with the inner part of the rock boot**

(Bottom) **Foot jam, with the big-toe side of the foot being pushed down to increase purchase**

crack at a slight angle, usually with the big-toe side of your foot lifted slightly, so that it touches both sides. Then straighten your foot so that your sole goes as flat as possible. This causes the rubber to grip the crack sides and give you purchase. Smaller width cracks can be climbed using a variation, the toe jam. Execution is exactly the same, with the twisting effect holding you in place. It should be said that toe jamming, when wearing thin, flexible climbing boots, is one of the less pleasant methods available!

Heel hook

This is potentially a fairly dynamic method of climbing over a roof, particularly one with a flat top, as well as being useful for performing partial or extreme versions of a move known as a 'rock-over' (see below). The appropriate foot is lifted up and the heel placed onto the hold. This has the effect of removing a lot of weight from your arms, making it easier to pull yourself up. As you do so you will usually have to either move towards your foot, ending up 'rocking over' onto it, or keep moving it towards you as you get higher, ending up with your sole flat on the hold. A heel hook can also be used in a similar fashion to a toe hook (see below), where it is placed around a suitable hold to help keep you in place and prevent you from 'barn-dooring' (pivoting) off.

Toe hook

This is commonly used to help keep you in position, to prevent the 'barn-dooring' mentioned above. This can happen when, for instance, you have one foothold directly underneath you, with both handholds together and off to one side, thus throwing you off balance. A toe hook can be used to help you to remain stable, as you can place it around a suitable hold to counter any rotation.

SPECIFIC CLIMBING STYLES

Layaway

This is a most useful technique and is very common. It allows you to move up past areas of blank rock to reach better holds higher up. It is predominantly a balance move and uses holds in opposition, and as such should be practised a number of times using a variety of holds and distances.

We will assume that you have come across a short crack with a blank section above, requiring you to reach higher than you think possible.

1   Holding onto the crack, lean off to one side and move your feet up as high as possible. If the footholds are directly underneath the crack there is a chance of you 'barn-dooring' off, so place your outer foot across and ahead of you, and press it inwards onto the rock. This will stop you rotating out and off.

2   Pulling into the crack, straighten the supporting leg (underneath you) and reach up with one hand for the higher hold.

(Above) **Heel hooking in preparation for a rock-over**

(Below) **A composite photo of a layaway. Note the leg out in front, stopping the climber from barn-dooring at the start. Reaching up for the good hold, pull in with one hand and push up with the supporting leg.**

Laybacking

This is almost like a series of layaways linked together in order to gain height. It uses holds in opposition and is quite tiring over any distance, especially if the handholds are difficult to use, perhaps being rounded. It is, however, an effective way of climbing and successful completion owes as much to technique as to strength.

Let's assume that you are going to climb a section of crack whose edges are about 30cm apart.

1   Grip one edge with your hands and place your feet against the other edge.
2   Move one hand up a little and then the other, then do the same for your feet.
3   Make the most of any irregularities for your feet to adhere to, and feel carefully with your hands for the best edge section to grip.

Bridging

This is a very useful way of ascending chimneys and corners, and need not be tiring as most of your bodyweight will be on the legs. It can rely on friction, but will often make the most of small holds such as incuts and pebbles. The technique is simply to have one hand and one foot on one section of wall, the other hand and foot on the other section. These are moved up in turn as appropriate, and there is no particular sequence to be followed. For instance, you may move hand-hand-foot-foot for a distance and then change to hand-foot-foot-hand, depending on your balance and the frequency (or not) of good holds.

Back and footing

This is a method of climbing chimneys or very wide cracks, and can feel very secure.

1   Place both feet on one wall of the chimney, your back and hands on the other.
2   To ascend, bend one knee and have the foot on the wall directly beneath you. Push the palms of your hands against the wall behind you and, keeping both feet in opposition, move your body up a distance.

(Opposite) **Laybacking up 'Pedestal Crack', Diff, Swanage**

(Above) **Bridging**

(Below) **Back and footing**

3 Lean back against the wall, place your underneath supporting foot across and next to the other, and move your legs up by 'walking' them higher. Take care at this point: all your weight will be supported by one leg as the other moves.

4 Repeat the process – moving up feet then back – until you have gained the height you want. It is quite common, on extended chimney routes, to combine this technique with bridging, changing over as and when necessary.

Mantelshelves

This is employed for climbing onto a ledge where there are no useful holds for some distance above, and often used to gain the flat ground at the top of a route. If the ledge is wide an ungraceful belly flop will often solve the problem, albeit most likely to the derisive hoots of your watching companion! Better to do it in style and, if faced with a large ledge to gain, this can be fairly simple.

1 Get yourself in a position where you can push yourself up so that you are supported by your arms, which will be pushing straight down on to the ledge, fairly near the edge.

2 Lift up one leg and place your foot flat on the ledge, slightly off to one side.

3 Manoeuvre your bodyweight so that it is over this foot, and use your leg muscles to stand up straight. You will find that it is helpful for the other foot (hanging down below the ledge) to be used in a 'dabbing' motion against the rock, thus taking a bit off weight off the supporting leg and making standing up easier. With a bit of luck there will be a hold a short distance above the ledge that you can use to help lift up your weight whilst pushing with your leg.

It is very common to solve a mantelshelf problem by pushing up with your arms and then, instead of lifting a foot up, putting a knee on to the ledge. Although some climbers would exclaim at this blatant display of lack of flexibility, if it solves the problem and makes you more secure, go for it. It does, however, have a couple of drawbacks.

- If the ledge is very narrow it can be awkward to then lift your leg up to stand on your feet.
- Placing one or both knees on to a ledge with an uneven surface hurts! However, if you are faced with the problem and using your knees will solve it, that's fine.

Performing a mantelshelf on to a narrow ledge will take quite a bit of practice and leg strength, along with a large amount of balance. Your body will have to be orientated more sideways than full on, and good flexibility will be the key to success.

Rock-over

A rock-over is where you move your bodyweight across and onto a foot prior to standing up on it, in order to reach holds some way above. It is almost like a version of a mantelshelf, although it will be approached slightly differently.

1   Using whatever holds are available for your hands, work your feet up until the one to be used can be placed onto the hold out to one side.
2   Now 'rock over' on to it, using a combination of balance, leg strength, available handholds and your lower foot dabbing upwards against the rock. Once you are well in balance you can think about reaching up for the higher handhold.

Mantelshelf

Dynos

This is short for 'dynamic', and is where the climber's body is accelerated up past its normal balance point in order to grab a higher hold. There are three versions: a 1st-generation dyno has one hand off the starting hold with the other still gripping it; a 2nd-generation has both hands off; a 3rd-generation has both hands and both feet off the rock!

The first type will be used most often, as the latter two require you to reach whatever you are going for successfully – if you don't, you're off! The skill with the first is in being able to make the move and, if you do not succeed first time, being able to bring yourself back down and into balance before trying again. Having confidence in your starting position is important, as is knowing how to use the holds that you'll be using to propel yourself up.

Another important aspect of any type of dyno is the 'dead point'. This is the point at which your body ceases its upward motion and loses momentum, pausing for the briefest of moments before gravity starts pulling it down again. The trick is to be able to grip the hold when you are at the dead point; this will make holding onto it successfully a

(Above left)
Making a 'dyno' move

(Above right)
Resting on a straight arm

lot easier and also goes a long way towards preventing soft tissue injury. To grab for a hold as you are descending past it, with your body accelerating, is asking to pull a tendon or cause similar damage.

Resting

The most obvious rest is going to be when you come across a ledge you can stand on in balance, but don't wait until you are tired before looking for one. Make the most of any opportunity for a breather before you get worn out. However, since there won't always be a ledge exactly where you want one, you need to have another plan.

A straight-arm hang is the commonest form of resting your hands, and allows one arm at a time to be shaken out and given time to recover. A straight arm will be better than a bent one, as you will be resting on bone as opposed to trying to keep yourself on with tired muscles. Select the best hold nearby and don't be afraid to bend your knees, using any small purchase for your feet, so that your arm is in the best position. Swap hands whenever you need to so that both can be shaken out.

Resting using a knee bar

It may be possible to get a hands-off rest. You will need to be wedged in a certain position or jam a body part, such as your shoulder or hips, into a suitable crack in the rock. This will allow you to get both arms down by your side, giving you maximum rest potential.

If you are feeling very athletic, it is possible to use all sorts of things to jam into the rock so that you can get a breather. The photograph shows a knee bar being used, but a hanging foot jam could also be done here. Not for the faint-hearted, these are only really of use at the very highest levels, or as a party trick to impress your friends!

Making moves over specific obstacles

These are the basic moves, and many more will come naturally. You need to work on your skill base so that you can decide what technique is appropriate, not forgetting that you will probably approach and solve the same problem in a totally different manner to your partner. Below is a reminder of how to solve a few of the problems listed above, bearing in mind that each case – and each climber – will be different.

(Above left) **Slab**
(Above right) **Steep wall**
(Below) **Crack**

- **Slab** You will be climbing in balance, keeping your body upright and getting a lot of boot rubber in contact with the rock. A relaxed posture and manner are the keys to success; if you are tense you tend to hunch over, spoiling the fine balance that is needed to climb well. Keep a lookout for irregularities in the surface that will give your feet a little more purchase.

- **Steep wall** This requires some strength and stamina, especially if it is near vertical. The steeper it becomes the more sideways your posture will be, helping you to maintain your balance more easily. Edging with your boots on incuts and effective crimping or pulling on pebbles will help to get you up.

- **Crack** A thin line will require the use of finger and hand jams, along with foot jams of various types. It may be that there is enough friction either side of the crack for your feet to find purchase, using just your hands for jamming. If the crack is wide, laybacking will be the solution, working your hands and feet up in opposition, making use of any respite that may present itself.

- **Corner** If it has a crack running down it, you are spoilt for choice. Jamming, laybacking, bridging and simply climbing up using holds on either side will do the job, with any combination being used to gain height.

- **Chimney** This can be climbed by back and footing or bridging, but remember that the interior of the chimney may be well furnished with 'normal' holds, allowing you to simply climb up as usual, making the most of both sides.

- **Bulge or roof** Both of these may require a bold approach, depending on their size and the availability of holds. Mantelshelves, rock-overs and layaways may all have to be deployed. You will normally have to work your feet up as high as possible then reach over for the next available hold. If a crack splits the roof (as is often the case) finger, hand or fist jamming could be the answer.

(Above) **Corner**
(Below left) **Chimney**
(Below right) **Roof**

MOVING ON ROCK

7 PLACING GEAR

This is probably the most important aspect of ensuring a safe climb, whether leading, top- or bottom-roping, or belaying. The ability to spot a potential placement, decide upon and select the right piece of gear, seat it properly, connect the rope and continue on, very often all done with one hand, takes a long time to master. Practice always makes perfect and, in this case, could also save your life – or that of your partner.

ASSESSING PLACEMENTS

It is important to have some means of assessing the soundness of a placement and the likelihood of it pulling out under load. A useful system is to rate everything on a scale of 1–5, where 1 is poor and 5 is as good as it gets. This can be used to assess individual placements on the lead, and will help you to develop an understanding of what is good and what is not.

It's handy to allocate a total score of at least 10 to an anchor set-up. If you are building up a belay system out of two wires, both of which have a '5' rating, this totals 10 and it's probably safe to go. However, if you only rate your two wires as 3 and 4, thus making 7, you need another piece of gear in to reach (or exceed) your target of 10. The only anomaly here is that I would rate slings as being up to 10 in one go; you might place a really good sling around a large boulder or tree trunk and just belay from that one point. However, it would be a 'bold' decision (a very polite way of putting it!), to belay from a single wire – and so not recommended – hence the minimum of doubling them up. Camming devices are not appropriate for use in anchor set-ups as they cannot be relied upon to remain in one position.

SLINGS

These are perhaps the easiest gear placements to make, but are often neglected. They can be arranged over spikes or threaded through holes in the rock or between boulders, generally making a very strong and secure running belay or anchor. The 8ft (120cm) slings are often the most useful here, although shorter and longer ones should not be ignored.

> **Note**
>
> Camming devices have the ability to 'walk' into a crack. Because of this, if they are used as part of an anchor system and the rope moves, the cam may move enough to alter the loading on the separate sections of the system, loading it unevenly. A cam could also move so much that it releases itself entirely from its placement. If you have a '10' rated anchor and need to be slightly to one side of it for the **ABC** to be correct, you could use a cam to bring you into line. However, I would choose to use a wire or chock wherever possible and avoid cams altogether.

Spike belay or runner

This is where the sling can be placed over a projecting nose of rock in such a way that it cannot be pulled off. The direction of loading should be carefully considered, as should the effect of the rope flicking the sling.

If the sling is too long, you could tie an overhand knot in it to achieve the appropriate length and clip the karabiner in above that. Alternatively, it could be wrapped around the spike twice, with the karabiner being clipped through both loops. Don't be tempted to just clip into one, as the tightening effect could cause the sling to inch its way up and off the spike over time.

(Left) **Spike runner**

(Middle) **Spike runner with the sling shortened using an overhand knot**

(Right) **Spike runner with the sling wrapped around twice and the karabiner clipped into both loops**

Note

If you are concerned about the sling staying on the spike, as you feel that the movement of the rope may cause it to lift or jiggle off, weighing it down may help to keep it in place. This can be done with some extra gear being clipped to it to keep it hanging straight. Take care, though, that you do not leave behind anything that may be needed later on the pitch (very difficult to judge), with perhaps a couple of extenders being the best kit to sacrifice.

Thread runner

A big advantage of a thread is that it will take a load in any direction. This is important if it is being used to direct the rope up the line of a route, where the belayer has to stand

(Right)
Thread runner clipped correctly

(Far right)
**Thread runner tied off with a
lark's-foot – to be avoided**

some distance back. If being used as a runner, it also stops any concerns about the rope flicking the sling off its perch.

In some rock types – such as limestone and sandstone – there may be natural threads through the rock, the hole having been caused by water erosion or the long-term removal of a soft layer behind a harder one. However, most of the time a thread will be fashioned at the point where two rocks are butted together, or where a jammed rock in a crack or chimney allows the sling to be wrapped around it. Another common style of thread will be around a tree root, trunk or branch.

When threading a sling in this way, don't be tempted to lark's-foot it (where one side of the sling is pushed through the other), as this makes a weak knot that could cause the sling to tighten around the thread and become irretrievably jammed between the boulders, or even lever them apart. Instead, simply clip the two ends together.

Pre-placed stakes
Some crags, in particular those with sandy or grassy tops such as sea cliffs, will have pre-placed gear left *in situ*, most often in the form of metal stakes driven in just back from the vertical. You need to be sure that the stake is sound, particularly in a saline environment where it could be rusting through just below the surface. It would always be prudent to use them in pairs, or back them up with another type of anchor. When putting a sling over a stake, it would be a

Clove hitch on a stake, with a wrap being taken around the back

good idea to use a clove hitch. To ensure added security, take one side of the sling and wrap it around the back of the stake, which has the effect of inverting the clove hitch and making it lock off tight. There is now little chance of the sling lifting off unexpectedly.

WIRES

The range of wire sizes varies considerably, but their placement, at least for modern curved-section wires, remains essentially the same across the board. There are a number of specialist wires with complicated uneven trapezoid cross-sections, and these tend to be in the smaller size ranges. They can be categorised as additions to a standard rack when a specific purpose is intended, such as the protection of a very hard route with placements composing of thin, unhelpful cracks. For the purposes of this book we will concentrate on standard wire shapes, with one convex and one concave side.

Wire placement

Wires can be placed into either horizontal or vertical cracks. An ideal placement will be where a vertical crack starts wide and narrows towards the bottom, with the back being a little wider than the front. This allows the wire to sit in a very strong position; it will not only take a high loading but will also be resistant to being flicked out by the movement of the rope.

Note

You may be carrying 8ft (120cm) and 16ft (240cm) slings around your body with a screwgate attached to each, which is very sensible. This means that there will be a screwgate on any sling that has been placed on the lead. As far as security is concerned, it will be worth taking an extra couple of seconds to spin the locking sleeve shut, as long as it is convenient to do so. If, however, you are not feeling too secure when placing the sling and you can only just manage to clip it, you may elect to carry on with the gate undone, treating it in the same manner as a snapgate.

When you place a wire, select it from the group on the karabiner, place it into the crack, hold onto the others and give them a smart tug downwards to seat the wire in place. You do this to increase the security of the placement, not to see if it will hold in the event of being loaded. You will never recreate the forces of a fall just by pulling, and you should be able to tell if the crack is suitable or not just by looking at its shape.

When you do tug, make sure that it is in the direction of loading so that the head of the wire sits in the correct orientation. Never tug with both hands; if the wire did come out for some reason you would be thrown off balance and might fall. Always make sure that one hand has a good hold on the rock.

(Above) **Perfect wire placement**

(Below left) **Wire sitting in a stable position in a near-parallel-sided crack**

(Below right) **Wire being used sideways in a flared crack**

Less-than-perfect placements

Sadly, perfect placements don't crop up constantly and we need to use a bit of cunning when protecting a route, or when constructing a belay anchor. Luckily, modern-day wires are constructed very scientifically and can cope with a variety of placement types. Their convex/concave shape means that they only need three points of contact around the head to render them stable, a distinct advantage over older, straight-sided versions. Additionally, the concave side may be a little narrower than the convex one, allowing the wire to be seated in flared cracks.

(Left) **Wire placed into a horizontal crack with the convex side of the head down**

Horizontal placements

Wires can also be used in horizontal cracks, ideally where a protrusion from the top of the crack sits into the concave part of the wire head. In any case, they should be placed with the convex side down. In the event of loading this causes the head to rock on its rounded side, jamming itself into the placement even tighter.

Extending the wire

If a wire is being placed on the lead, an extender should be used to stop any chance of the movement of the rope unseating it. Ensure that the extender is long enough to bring the rope into line with other runners on the route – using a sling may sometimes be necessary if the wire is placed some way to one side. If the wire is being used as part of an anchor system, such as when setting up a belay in order to bring up your second, a screwgate karabiner should be used to provide maximum security.

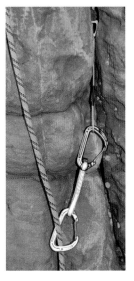

(Above) **Extender on a wire**

(Below) **Wire threaded through a gap**

> ## Tip
> If you ever 'thread' a wire into a placement, be sure to tell your second how you did it to avoid him spending hours trying to work out how to retrieve it in the conventional manner!

Threading a wire

Occasionally it may be possible to thread a wire though a natural hole in the rock, or through a gap between a couple of boulders. Simply unclip the relevant wire from the carrying karabiner and poke the loop end through the hole. Clipping an extender to this makes the whole set-up very secure. Although the wire may rattle about there is no way that it can ever fall out.

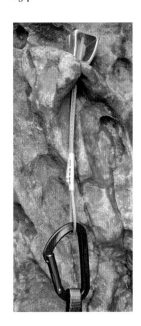

Two wires in opposition, with
the connecting sling tied off
around one with a clove hitch

Wires placed in opposition

In some extreme circumstances it may be necessary to place two wires in opposition to each other. In other words, when they are loaded they pull together rather than pull outwards, thus remaining in place. This is most commonly seen on horizontal placements, where a single wire (or a larger chock, as described below) will not work with a direct outwards pull and needs to be redirected. These pieces of gear can be connected by looping an extender through a karabiner on the other, or by tying them in place with a clove hitch. This second method is usually preferable, as it helps to keep the wires in position and lessens the chance of them being loosened or flicked out by the rope.

> ### Tip
>
> The very first wire placement, if it is close to the ground, may be better off without an extender on it. A spare karabiner clipped directly into it will suffice, with the advantage that it will give you an extra few inches of protection. This may make the difference between your ankle hitting the ground or not in the event of a slip.

> ### Note
>
> It is essential that a karabiner is used to connect the rope to the wire, and is not just threaded through – the same goes for attaching a sling. In the event of loading, the very thin wire could cut right through a rope or sling, with disastrous consequences.

> ### Tip
>
> Most climbers will carry a selection of wires on one karabiner. Should the first size you try be too small/large the next size up or down will be immediately to hand. My preference is to have sizes 1–6 on one karabiner, 7–10 on another. These would usually be doubled up, so I'd have 12 on one krab and eight on the other, with the reasoning that the larger sizes are heavier and bulkier so fewer on a single krab works well.

Note

Keep a check on your wires to make sure that they do not become abraded. If this happens (you will soon be able to tell as you will probably catch your finger on the offending spike of wire) it must be retired from use immediately. A loss of a strand means a loss in strength for the complete unit, and this cannot be risked.

Tip

When packing your wires into a rucksack, lay them down sideways. If you just drop them in vertically they could become bent and distorted under the weight of other gear sitting on top.

ROCKCENTRICS AND OTHER LARGE METAL CHOCKS ON ROPE OR TAPE

This style of chock relies on the differential in the size of its sides to provide a rotating and camming action when loaded along the correct axis. Generally speaking, the harder you pull the more secure the placement. They can be placed in a variety of positions, the options being clarified on the manufacturer's instructions.

This style of chock can also be used as a simple jamming device. If there is a gap in the rock, perhaps where two solid boulders are very close together, the chock can be placed behind them. Although not camming as designed, there is no way that it will pull out – the metal head is simply too large to pull through.

(Right) **Rockcentric placed correctly in a tapering crack, with the widest side in contact**
(Below left) **Rockcentric camming in an alternative manner**
(Below right) **Rockcentric placed in a large gap, loose but with no way of being pulled out with a downwards loading**

(Left) **Rockcentric being used in a horizontal crack**
(Right) **Rockcentric side-on in a suitable crack**

When used in a horizontal placement, the rounded side is usually best positioned downmost.

When viewing some chock faces from the front, you will notice that the lower section is slightly narrower than the top. This allows the chock to be placed across a suitably narrowing crack line. Make sure that it is seated properly along the edges and cannot easily be flipped out by the rope.

CAMMING DEVICES

These will make up the most expensive part of your lead kit, and are by far and away the least understood and most abused part of a rack. If poorly placed they have a propensity to jam and will refuse to come out again. Crags worldwide show evidence of poor cam placements with the stubby ends of stems and sun-bleached bits of tape protruding from them.

Most designs work on a similar system, somewhat akin to a hypodermic syringe. Your thumb sits on the end of the central bar or wire loop, with either one or two fingers – depending upon the design – placed a little further down on a trigger bar or loop. Squeezing thumb and fingers together causes the cams to retract.

Problems can arise if cams are placed incorrectly:

- When cams are jammed into a crack that is too small for them. As soon as they are in and the trigger released, it becomes impossible to retrieve them.
- Having the cams too wide open also causes problems, as they don't have enough leverage left when loaded and can pull straight out.
- It is therefore important that they are only placed into cracks that will accept them when they are working in their mid-70 percent operating range, neither too open nor closed too tightly.

Once you have retracted the cams and placed the device into a crack, a little space either side will be fine. However, if you let the trigger go and the cams open out to 90 degrees from the stem that is too wide. Practice is important, as is studying the manufacturer's instructions.

If you are placing the unit into a vertical crack and it doesn't seem to fit particularly well one way, take it out, turn it round 180 degrees and try it again. As the cams on one side of the unit are spaced wider than those on the other, trying different positions should eventually give you the best placement.

Horizontal cam placements
Cams with flexible stems are well suited to placements in horizontal cracks. They should be initially positioned with the wider apart cams downmost, as this will make them more stable. However, you may find that in some cases, as in a vertical crack, they sit better the other way up. Ensure that the flexible part of the stem is at the point where it will easily run down and over the lower edge of the crack in the event of a fall.

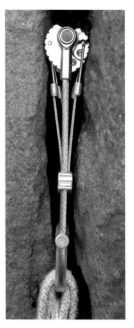

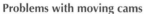

(Above) **Camming device placed correctly into a vertical crack**

(Left) **Cam in a horizontal placement**

Problems with moving cams
'Walking' is something that affects most cams. As each element is normally sprung independently, given a bit of movement on the stem (such as the motion of the rope flicking too and fro) the device can 'walk' deeper into the crack. This can cause a number of problems:

- It could walk in a long way and become irretrievable.
- It may go to a point where the crack widens and the unit opens out and becomes useless.
- It may make its way in and get tighter and tighter, finally jamming solid.

If there is any chance of a cam being affected by the rope and moving, clip an extender or short sling to its sewn tape loop. Some designs have a doubled-up sewn loop as standard, and this may be long enough to overcome the problem when clipped singly.

Cam extended to avoid it 'walking'

Alternative method of placing cams
Some designs have 'stops' on the sides of each individual cam section. This allows them to be placed in a wide-open position, in much the same manner as a passive nut. It is not very likely that you will have to do this, as there will be other gear on your rack that will do the job better, but it is worth knowing that it is a possibility.

Tip

Make the most of those wet and windy days, or when you have no climbing partner, by getting out onto the crag – not to do a route, but to practise your gear placement skills. Time spent on a non-climbing day, simply walking along the foot of a cliff and placing gear when the opportunity presents itself, will repay itself many times when you actually need it. Make it realistic and rack up a harness, placing gear with one hand in order to get the feel. Some bouldering areas are good for this practice, as you can be just a little way off the ground when placing gear, making the process realistic.

7

PLACING GEAR

8 BELAYING

Although there are many different ways to belay, this chapter covers the tried and tested techniques that, if carried out correctly, will go a long way to ensuring the security of both you and your climbing partner.

ABC

This fundamental requirement needs to be understood and carried out in order for belaying to be carried out in as safe a manner as possible. It is a mental check every time you tie onto an anchor, ready to belay your partner. It is not only relevant to those belaying at the top of a route, but is also important if a ground anchor is being taken at the bottom.

Remember that:

A = anchor
B = belayer
C = climber

All three must be tight and in line; remember this every time you anchor. If the belayer (**B**) is not tight on the anchor (**A**), in the event of a fall he will get pulled forwards. If the rope to the climber (**C**) is not in line via the belayer (**B**) to the anchor (**A**), the belayer will be pulled sideways when the system is loaded.

Remember that the line between anchor and belayer must be straight, not only in the horizontal plane but also in the vertical. If the anchor is low down and the belayer is standing up, he has a chance of being pulled forwards and downwards when loaded and subsequently losing his footing. Sitting down to belay will always be the most stable position, but if you have to stand make sure that the anchors are above hip height behind you.

| **Well-positioned and braced belayer, with the ABC correct** | **Poor ABC: in the event of a fall the belayer will be pulled forwards** | **ABC off-line: when loaded, the belayer will be pulled over to the side** |

TYPES OF BELAY METHOD

There are two types of belay method relevant here, the 'semi-direct' and the 'direct'. The 'directness' element indicates how much of the load is taken by the anchor system.

- **Semi-direct belay** Probably the most common, where the belay device is clipped onto a rope loop on the belayer's harness. This makes it 'semi-direct' as far as the anchor is concerned, because the load will also be partially shared by the belayer, not least due to the fact that the belayer will naturally tend to lean back a little to hold any weight.
- **Direct belay** All the load goes straight onto the anchor, with the belayer not part of the process in any way, other than holding the dead rope.

How do you choose between the two types? Most climbers will find that a semi-direct belay, with the device being clipped on in front at around waist height, will be easy to handle and manipulate, as well as being very quick to set up. It can deal with all situations, and is quite easy to operate. The direct belay is also quick to set up, with one major consideration: any anchor used must be totally solid, and there can be no question about its ability to remain fast under a load. If the anchor should fail, the result will be disastrous.

Note

There is a third method, the 'indirect' belay. This is where the load is taken around the body of the belayer, who will be using a 'classic or 'waist belay' system of taking the rope in. This means that any loading is taken fully around the body, which can be extremely painful if a fall of any distance has to be held, and is potentially very dangerous to both belayer and climber. The old-fashioned way of belaying, it still has its place in some situations, such as when snow and ice anchors are being used. As far as its role in modern rock climbing is concerned we will pursue it no further.

SEMI-DIRECT BELAY

This will usually be the automatic first choice for anyone belaying a climbing partner. There are a few plus and minus points to consider, the most important of which are outlined below.

8

BELAYING

Pros

- The device can be easily and quickly clipped into the tie-in loop on the harness.
- Relatively simple to learn to operate correctly.
- Gives a good amount of control when taking in and paying out.
- Easy to give a helping 'tug' to someone on a top or bottom rope.

Cons

- Belayer is part of the system, thus is pulled around in the event of a fall.
- ABC critical, especially at the top of a route.

Note

It is important to understand the difference between the 'live' rope and the 'dead' rope.

- The 'live' rope leads from your belay device directly to the climber. You can remember it as it has a live person on the end.
- The 'dead' rope is the one coming out of the belay device and onto the pile of rope on the ground. It is this rope that must be always held and controlled correctly, as it provides the braking and lowering capability of the whole system. Although it is so called as it leads to unused, in other words 'dead', rope on the ground, perhaps a better – if gruesome – way to remember it is that if you let go, your partner is dead.

Clipping a belay device onto your harness

Usually when out with a partner and leading routes you will be tied onto the end of the rope from the word go, and the belay device will be attached onto the rope loop at your harness. However, there will be times when you are not tied on, and will then be belaying from the abseil loop. This is not recommended for any situation where the rope is likely to be shock loaded in any way, as might happen when belaying a leader who may fall. Belaying on a bottom-rope system is one instance where you may have the device clipped directly to the abseil loop, as the climber will not fall any distance but simply dangle. Most of the time, though, you will have the rope tied on, and we will concentrate on this system.

When you are belaying a leader the device will be clipped onto the top of the tie-in loop. Make sure that it is oriented in the correct manner, with the braking hand holding the dead rope downwards and the rope to the leader coming out of the top of the device.

When at the top of a route and belaying a second, the device is clipped to the bottom section of the tie-in loop. The braking hand is at the top of the device, with the rope to the climber coming out from the bottom.

(Above left) **Belay device correctly clipped in and oriented for belaying a leader**

(Above right) **Belay device clipped in and oriented correctly for belaying a second**

How to belay

Managing the rope to a leader does appear to be a simple process initially, but it takes practice to get it right. There will be a certain amount of taking in and paying out, and doing this properly is key to being a safe and effective belayer.

The maximum friction possible will be achieved with the dead rope held at 180 degrees to the live rope, in other words in a straight line. Minimum friction is achieved by bringing your braking hand holding the dead rope to the front of the device, so that the two sections of rope are now parallel. In practice you will rarely need to do this, as you will soon be able to lessen the friction by easing your braking hand towards the device from the rear, without taking the risk of bringing it all the way forward.

Tip

Always take a moment to check for twists in the rope, and ensure that it is all running in the correct orientation. If the rope crosses over itself and you start to belay it could become jammed in the slots of the device when loaded, becoming almost impossible to dislodge.

Paying out to a leader:
- Hold the dead rope with your hand a little behind your hip.
- Your other hand holds the live rope just in front of the device, grips the rope and pulls through the required amount.
- The dead rope hand can move forwards with the rope, feeding it in, always keeping hold in case the leader slips.
- When enough rope has been paid through, the braking hand can be slid back carefully down the rope to its original position.
- The hand on the live rope returns to just in front of the device.

Taking in the rope when belaying a second from the top of a route involves a slightly different process:
- Start with one hand quite a distance in front of the device on the live rope, the other hand just behind the device on the dead rope.
- As the second climbs up, move the braking hand forwards to the front of the device at the same time as pulling up with the live rope hand. It is important to

Note

When selecting a belay position it is important to think about the movement of your arm during the belaying process. If you are near any rock bulges or wedged into a chimney it will be difficult getting your braking arm into the correct position swiftly for arresting a fall.

coordinate your hands so that no slack rope collects between them. Your braking hand will travel the same distance as the live rope hand, and for a moment the live and dead ropes will be parallel.

- Now bring your braking hand back to your side, creating the 180 degree angle required to lock off the device.
- The hand on the live rope can now let go and be brought up to your side and placed on to the dead rope, just in front of your other hand.
- This now lets go and moves forward, to grip the dead rope just behind the device.
- The other hand now lets go and is placed back on the live rope, ready to repeat the process.

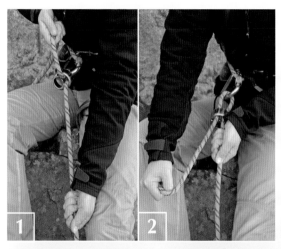

STEP 1
Hands in the braking position

STEP 2
Taking in the rope

STEP 3
Locking off the rope and swapping hands

STEP 4
Bring the rear hand in front of the other one

STEP 5
Back to the original position

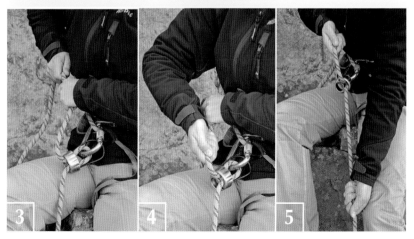

Tip

When belaying, either paying in or taking out, don't let your hand get close to the belay device. It is quite possible to catch a piece of skin, often the bit between thumb and forefinger, in the device and then be trapped between it and the rope – a rather unpleasant experience!

Note

Be very careful if using thin ropes – especially new ones with a dry-treated surface – in conjunction with a belay device that has large diameter holes through which the rope passes. Holding a fall can be very difficult, and loss of control is a real possibility. It is worth having a device that can cope with thin ropes, which will normally mean purchasing one with grooved channels on the dead rope side to provide extra friction.

This method of belaying is very secure as it guarantees that at least one hand is always on the dead rope, ready to hold on in the event of the climber falling. This will also be the same process for belaying on a bottom rope, with the obvious difference that you will have the rope coming down towards you, rather than coming up the crag.

DIRECT BELAY

One of the big advantages of this method is that you are out of the system; if your partner takes a fall you are not subjected to any loading. It has, therefore, got its place in a situation where a number of falls might be taken. This is most likely in a top-roping situation where your partner is climbing something far harder than his normal grade, perhaps for training purposes. In these circumstances it may be less harrowing and demanding for the belayer to utilise a direct belay system. Note however that it takes a lot of judgement to set up and a little more experience to handle safely. The main good and bad points are outlined below:

Pros
- Belayer is out of the system, thus will not be pulled around in the event of the climber falling.
- Belayer is able to position himself at the optimum point for controlling the system, which could be some way in front of it.
- Quick and easy to set up.

Cons
- Anchor must be totally solid, with no question whatsoever about its holding power.
- Not appropriate for belaying a leader.
- Belayer, not being part of the system, needs to remember to attach himself to a part of the anchor.

Setting up a direct belay system

The most crucial part of setting up a direct belay system is to be 100 percent certain that the anchor is absolutely reliable. Having established that, the rest of the procedure is relatively straightforward. Instead of using a belay device we will use an Italian hitch with a direct system. This has a number of advantages, not least that you need to be in front of it for it to work properly, ideal when belaying from the top of the crag. Once the anchor has been selected, there are a number of options as to how to use it to its best advantage.

Simple direct belay for a top rope The simplest set-up will be a sling around an anchor, into which you – as well as the belaying karabiner – are clipped. This works well if the anchor is only a short distance, perhaps a couple of metres, away from the edge of the crag. The anchor – say a solid tree – has a sling placed around it, with your rope going to a karabiner on it for security. As the tree will be taking all the loading, it is not necessary to be very tight on this rope, and you can site yourself somewhere comfortable (remembering the the rope should not be too slack either). A second karabiner, an HMS, is also clipped into the sling (through the same section as yours) and an Italian hitch is clipped into this.

Simple direct belay, using a
sling around a spike

This method is quite useful if you are setting up a top-rope system. Should this be the case, you may not be tied into the end of the rope, as obviously you won't have led the climb. You could tie in and belay as above, or alternatively you could use a sling as a cow's-tail, threaded through the harness abseil loop, lark's-footed into place, and then clipped into the sling on the anchor. Ensure that the length of your sling is correct so that you can't fall over the edge, and shorten it with an overhand knot if necessary.

Sling being used as a cow's-tail

Belaying with a single anchor point If you are tied into the rope, such as after having led the route, there are alternatives. If you are using just one anchor point, or a couple equalised with a sling, the following will be a quick way of setting things up.

- Clip your rope into the anchor and make your way back to the edge of the crag, aware of your own security as you do so.
- Decide where you want to be to belay. Pull a little more slack through, perhaps 30–40cm, into the rope on your side of the anchor.
- Reaching back a little from the edge of the crag, hold both sides of the rope together so that they are tight on the anchor, with the slack you have just pulled through hanging in front of you.

- Tie an overhand knot on the bight at this point, around both ropes, treating them as one. This has the effect of a) tying you onto the anchor and b) creating a loop from which to belay.
- Clip an HMS into the loop, put an Italian hitch on it (after having pulled up all the slack), and belay from there.

This is a very quick and effective way of setting up a system, and after a little practice you will be able to judge the amount of slack to leave, which will let you tie the knot and end up positioned exactly where you want to be.

Belaying from two separate anchors If two separate anchors are being used, a similar system can be employed.

Tied onto an anchor and belaying from an overhand knot on the rope

- Clip the rope into both of the anchors.
- Make your way carefully to the edge of the cliff, pulling the rope from between the anchors with you. When in position the ropes will be making an 'M' shape.
- Give yourself some slack on your section of rope, and double the ropes back so that you have three loops lying on top of each other.
- Tie an overhand knot on the bight around these loops. This again creates a belay loop at the same time as securing you to the anchors.
- Clip an HMS karabiner into this loop and belay from there.

Although this may sound complicated it isn't in practice, and a little time spent getting it right will pay dividends – you will soon find that it can be set up quite quickly and efficiently.

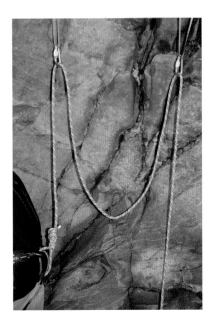 

(Left) **Setting up the loops from two anchors**

(Right) **The completed system**

How to belay

Belaying with an Italian hitch is quite straightforward. Maximum friction with the hitch is obtained with both live and dead ropes parallel, which is why we have been tying it a little way behind us at the belay stance. To hold the weight of a climber who has slipped, simply keep a tight grip on the dead rope. When in use, we don't need to move the ropes apart at all, just shuffle them forwards and back.

To take in the following is the most secure process:

- Place one hand on the dead rope near the hitch and the other on the live rope about an arm's length away.
- Pull the rope up with the live hand whilst pulling the slack through the hitch with the dead one. It is important that no loose rope ends up around the HMS, so keep your hands coordinated.
- Holding onto the dead rope, take your live hand off and place it on the dead rope between your other hand and the HMS.
- Now move the original dead rope hand to near the HMS, take the original live rope hand off and replace it on the live rope in the original position.
- You are now ready to take in again.

This is a secure method of taking in the rope, and ensures that the dead rope always has one hand on it. It may help

you to be positioned a little bit sideways when belaying, or even facing in towards the anchor.

Paying out is a very simple procedure:

* Place both hands on the dead rope.
* Feed the rope into the hitch, either by shuffling your hands forwards and back, or by swapping them over as the rope is paid out.

It is possible to safeguard a climber with a direct belay from the base of a crag when bottom-roping. Anchor selection is again paramount, but if this is in order the procedure is the same as above.

(Left) **Starting to take in with the Italian hitch**
(Right) **Swapping hands on the dead rope**

(Below) **The position for paying out rope**

> ## Tip
>
> Although you may see some people doing it, I would suggest that you *do not belay a leader* with a direct belay. The shock-loading created by holding his weight creates huge forces on the anchor, and the strength of the rope could be compromised within the turns of the hitch.

Note

The Italian hitch is a symmetrical knot, looking the same for taking in as it does for paying out. If you are changing from belaying up to lowering off, perhaps when using a bottom-rope system, the hitch rotates through the karabiner (hence using an HMS with a wide curve), reforming on the other side. If this is done under load it tends to 'pop' through, causing your climbing companion to assume wrongly that there is a problem, even though there isn't. Forewarn them if you don't want to hear them yelp!

Tip

If you drop your belay device and are left with just an HMS karabiner, it is fine to use an Italian hitch on your harness to bring up your second.

PART 3: CLIMBING

Placing gear on the lead

9 LEADING

LEARNING TO LEAD

Leading is one of the most difficult skills to get right, as so much depends on it. The bottom line is that you need to become competent at route finding, gear placement, belaying, ropework, stance management and so on, all of which takes time to put into place. It would be very easy to launch yourself at a climb armed with the best gear that money can buy, but unless you have carefully considered all the implications of everything you do, progress will be painfully slow – and possibly dangerous.

Leading on the atmospheric 'Second corner', Severe 4a, Swanage

Head games

So much of leading is about what goes on in your head. If we could do the same moves when leading as we might do at the climbing wall on a bottom rope, or when bouldering, global climbing grades would double overnight! If you ever watch the very best climbers, those right at the top of their sport, you will notice how focused they are. They mentally rehearse each move, often placing their hands on imaginary holds as they go through the sequence that will get them to the top. Often they will have practised the climb on a bottom rope, but leading a desperate route with minimal protection with a ground fall potential requires top-end mental strength and preparation.

When climbing a route as a second, a fall should result in nothing worse than a 'dangle' on the end of the rope. If you incur a fall when leading, however, you are almost certain to drop some distance, as your runners may be far below your feet. It is this possibility that defeats some people's leader aspirations.

Be positive

A positive mental attitude is needed. When you are ready to start, stand at the bottom of the climb, look up, and imagine how it will feel. Tell yourself that it will be a pushover, that you can't see any problems that will make the ascent difficult or scary. Imagine yourself at various points on the route and how you will feel, always in a positive manner. Saying 'I can do this' will automatically relax areas of the brain that would otherwise be telling you to go and do something else more sensible. As soon as you get on the rock, tell yourself how in control you are and how good you feel – all of this will give you a positive mental attitude for the rest of the route. Relax and enjoy it, as a relaxed climber will move well on the rock and often be able to climb a couple of grades harder than if tense.

Placing gear

The fear of falling greatly influences climbing ability. When you place a really good runner, tell yourself that there is no way that it will come out. Have a second look at it and reassure yourself that it is the best you've ever placed, and move on. Telling your belayer how good the gear is will also help to reaffirm the point in your own mind. Put it behind you, climb on and up and remain focused on the job in hand.

Coping with a fear of falling

Having no fear of falling is also something to work on. It is not human nature to enjoy dropping through the air, so we need to train ourselves to accept it as part of the deal of being a leader. Not that we ever intend to fall very often, but the potential is always there and we must be prepared.

Confidence in your belayer

Having a belayer whom you can trust is paramount. It doesn't matter if you can place the best gear in the world, if you have an inkling that your belayer may not be able to hold you if you drop, fear will set in and you are more likely to fail. Only time and your previous joint experience will tell you if your belayer is up to the job; if he is that's one thing less to worry about.

Falling off need not be as scary as it looks!

Practising falling

What does it feel like to fall? Most climbers will tell you that they hate the thought of falling, but are not sure exactly how it will feel. Find out for yourself. A good place is the local climbing wall where dynamic bottom ropes are set up to use. Climb partway up a route, have your belayer pay out a little slack and, once he is ready to hold you, drop off. It will seem like an anticlimax: nothing will break, bend or snap off. Try it again, perhaps with a little more slack this time. Still the same result. Now try leading a climb at the wall and take a short leader fall. This may be only a few centimetres but will still feel terrifying – until you've done it. A bit more of a drop this time? Nothing to it.

Unless you understand what it feels like to fall and be held, it will always remain a mystery and will sit as a lump of fear in the back of your mind. Try it out, unwrap the mystery, and you will find the result very positive.

Note

It may not be just you who is feeling nervous on a climb – bear a thought for your belayer. Often all the belayer can hear are grunting noises and strange mutterings, interspersed with 'oh no' and 'aarghhh'! It is quite scary looking up at a leader who you think is about to fall off, even though he may be completely in control. Keep your belayer informed of what is going on. In particular, if you get a good runner placement that you are happy with, let him know as well. This means that he can relax, safe in the knowledge that if you do fall you won't hit the ground in front of him.

PLACING RUNNERS

One of the most crucial skills to acquire is runner placement. To be able to place a good runner – and know that it's good – is a great morale booster and will help you to climb more confidently. There are safer options for practising placing gear (see below) than attempting to learn while leading a climb.

Deciding what makes a good runner involves many hours of practice trying out different bits of gear in different cracks, and a system for grading them is useful. The commonest is a scale of 1–5, where 1 is very poor and 5 is as good as it gets. Aim to have a 4 or 5 each time, which means that the chances of the runner pulling out under a fall situation are slight (see Chapter 7).

It is very important that you get into the habit of finding the piece of gear that suits the crack, not the other way round. It is tempting to stop at what looks to be a likely spot, select a piece of gear, perhaps a wire, and try to put it into a variety of different placements around and about. The real skill – which you will pick up quickly after a little

Note

It is important to clip the rope through the karabiner in the correct manner, so that it enters at the back next to the rock and runs up to your harness from the front. This is clarified under the back-clipping entry on page 121–2. Doing this incorrectly may leave you open to the danger of the rope unclipping itself from the karabiner in the event of a fall.

time practising – is to spot a placement, select the piece of gear efficiently, place it, clip it and move on. Knowing where your gear is racked on your harness is important, as is knowing which piece of gear is which size; most kit is colour-coded these days for this reason.

'Suspension', Severe 4a, Swanage – a steep climb, but with plenty of gear placements

Crag base practice

Walking along the base of a crag, looking for placements and putting in appropriate gear, is probably the best way to start. This allows you to see how each runner works, how to fit it in and tug it, and how to assess its qualities and security. It is far better to make a mistake here than when leading a route.

Have the gear racked on your harness as though you were doing it for real. You will soon learn where each piece of gear is and refine the system if necessary.

A good way to make progress is to traverse the base of the cliff just off the ground, in a suitable area with a safe landing. You have to make a variety of decisions, just as you would when leading:

- Where to stop to place the runner.
- Which hand to use (the other will probably be keeping you on the rock).
- Where the gear is on your harness and the best way to get to it.
- Think about body position and balance.
- After a bit of traversing, where is the best place to stop for a rest to let your arms recover.

This is extremely valuable experience and will closely mimic the real thing.

Top- and bottom-rope practice

The next stage is to try gear placement on a number of routes. A bottom or top rope will need to be set up at the appropriate place, and an understanding belayer. Climb the route and place gear as and when possible, but be careful to not use up everything over the first couple of metres! Once you have placed the gear, swap over and belay your partner. He then climbs the route and strips the gear out, but not before having a good look at your placements and commenting on their stability, how they could be improved and so on. You can then move onto another climb, perhaps with him taking the initiative next time.

You may wish to tow a spare rope up with you so that you can get into the habit of cleanly clipping each piece of gear. Alternatively, if you are bottom-roping and the route is not very long, you could use the other end of the rope with which you are being belayed. This is only possible if your partner is using his abseil loop to clip the belay device into, and cannot be done if he is also tied into the rope. It will also not be possible when you have rigged the bottom rope using the single-rope rigging system (see Chapter 13).

(Above) **Placing gear whilst traversing the base of a crag is very good practice – and quite realistic**

(Below) **Placing gear with the safety of a bottom rope**

If you are on your own and want to have a go at the gear game, select a suitable piece of crag and traverse just off the ground for a distance, say 10m. Step down and strip all the gear out, laying it off to one side. Now repeat the traverse, using what is left on your rack. Repeat until the placements are either no good or you have run out of gear.

THE GEAR GAME

This can teach you a lot about gear, and in particular how to be cunning when placing it. It is best done with someone else who is learning about leading, although you can do it on your own.

- Set up a top or bottom rope on a route; quite a short one will be fine.
- Set a limit to the amount of gear you are going to place – say five.
- You climb the route, placing gear as normal.
- You are lowered down, stripping the kit as you go.
- Putting your five used pieces to one side, hand the remainder of the rack over to your partner.
- He now climbs the route and places his choice of five pieces of gear.
- He takes out the gear as he descends, puts it to one side, passes what's left of the rack over to you, and so on.

The idea of this exercise is to make you think hard about where runners can be placed, and to make do with what is on your rack. Very often during your leading career you will be halfway up a route only to find that you have already used the runner you now need further down the climb. You will need to come up with an alternative, and this game will teach you to think about all possibilities.

LEADING ON A LOOSE BOTTOM ROPE

This is as close to leading as you can get without doing it for real. It is a method used by many instructors when teaching people to climb, as it mimics the feel of leading but with a safety back-up. It is best set up with a bottom rope as opposed to a top rope, as this makes belaying much easier to control.

Three people are needed:

- The climber
- Someone to belay the bottom rope
- The climber's belayer.

The bottom rope is rigged on an appropriate route, well within the climbing grade of whoever is going to lead and with plenty of opportunity to place runners. Note that the belayer who is holding the rope for the leader is now doing the job for real so must be positioned appropriately, and the use of ground anchors should be considered (see Chapter 10).

The climber – The idea is that the leader climbs the route, placing gear and clipping the rope in as he goes, exactly as he would do in real life. However, the bottom rope is there as a safety back-up. The climber is tied onto this as well, and the bottom-rope belayer takes in as the leader ascends. The difference is that – unlike normal bottom-roping where the rope is kept a bit snug between belayer and climber – the bottom rope is kept a little bit slack. It needs to be slack enough so that the situation feels realistic to the climber, but not so slack that he is in danger of hurting himself should he fall and a runner not hold. Reams of slack will also get in the way of the leader and could tangle or catch on the rock. About 1m may be appropriate, but every case will be different.

For example, as the leader leaves the ground and until he is 2–3m up the bottom rope must not have any slack in it. Should he fall he has a chance of hitting the deck and hurting himself, so the safety of the bottom rope is important. The higher he gets the more slack can be introduced into the system.

The bottom-rope belayer therefore plays a key role. Judging the amount of rope to keep in the system will need constant scrutiny. Apart from taking care near the ground, he is the back-up in the event of a fall. Thus, he needs to be in a suitable and braced position, and a ground anchor may also be relevant. Keeping alert and looking out for potential problems is also part of the job, perhaps spotting something that has been missed by the leader, such as a dislodged runner. In this case, the bottom rope will have to be quickly taken in snug.

It is comforting for the leader to know that, should he need help for any reason it can be activated very quickly. Perhaps fear has got the better of him, maybe the last runner wasn't quite as good as he thought; if for any reason the leader is unhappy he can call for the rope to be taken in tight and thus be supported from above.

The climber's belayer has an important job to do, exactly the same as if he were belaying a leader on his own. He should be positioned appropriately, handle the rope in the correct manner and be able to communicate and advise as required. This style of set-up is an excellent learning opportunity for him as well as for the leader; belaying someone above you for the first time can be a nerve-wracking experience, and knowing that there is a back-up relieves much of the pressure.

9

LEADING

Leading with a bottom-rope back-up

Once the leader has made it to the top, he can take off the bottom rope and drop it back down the crag. He can belay himself in an appropriate manner and bring up the second, who retrieves all the gear. The climb finishes exactly as if it is being led for real.

YOUR FIRST REAL LEAD

You and your partner are ready to do your first climb together. You are going to lead and your partner is going to belay. Which route are you going to do? A few considerations will affect your decision as to which route to climb, for example:

- A route that is within your ability, perhaps well below your current seconding grade, maybe even at the easiest level.
- A route that suits the experience of your belayer.
- A route that isn't too long. A shorter route will allow you plenty of opportunity to place gear but won't tire you out, enabling you to think more clearly.
- A climb that you want to do. If you don't like the look of it your mental preparation will be much harder and you may not enjoy the experience.
- A route with plenty of opportunities for gear placements; look out for good cracks or other similar features.
- Is your gear appropriate for the route? For instance, if it is a series of thin cracks is it a good idea to take a couple of size 11 rockcentrics? Alternatively, if all the runners appear to be threads and spikes, and you only have three slings between you, will you be able to protect it adequately?
- The bottom of the route should be appropriate and safe for your belayer, possibly with ground-anchor potential.
- The top of the route should have a variety of anchors that can be used by the climber to belay on, prior to bringing up the second.
- The descent to the bottom of the crag should be safe and not present any major problems.

Having checked through this list you will be in a good position to start. Take some time to help get your belayer sorted out, and make sure that he is also happy with your choice of climb.

Racking gear

Most climbers will clip their gear to the gear loops found on the majority of harnesses. However, some like to carry a bandolier across their chest with the rack, or at least part of it, clipped on. This comes down to personal preference but I feel that with a bandolier the gear gets crunched up and difficult to get hold of, especially when on a tricky section of route and trying to extract a piece of gear with one hand. I also feel that it swings me off balance when negotiating roofs and bulges, as it is quite heavy and can pivot around my body with quite a high mass. Having said that, a regular climbing partner of mine clips all his extenders to a bandolier and the rest of the rack to his harness, a hybrid system. A bandolier may also be useful when you progress to multi-pitch routes, as it can make the swapping over of gear at stances a little quicker and easier.

(Above) **Gear racked on a bandolier**

Racking gear onto a harness

We will assume that you are going to use the harness gear loops for everything. Hopefully when practising gear placements you will have come up with a system of racking that works for you. As a right-hander I prefer to have most of the protection on my right-hand side on a four-gear loop harness. I start with small wires then big, then onto cams, again running from small to big. Behind these, and probably on the rear right-hand loop (with the larger cams) I'll have any rockcentrics or large chocks. I put extenders on the front left-hand loop, with the rear left loop being used for sundry bits and pieces, such as the belay device, spare screwgates (it's worth carrying two for belaying), and prusik loops if appropriate. The important thing is to have a system that works for you, where you can locate and unclip any gear that is needed swiftly and effectively.

(Below) **Gear racked on harness gear loops**

(Right) **Clipping upwards onto a gear loop**

(Above) **Clipping up a rockcentric to prevent it swinging around**

Tip

Think ahead as to what gear you are going to need on the climb. If it is a slab covered in lots of thin cracks carrying a selection of large camming devices and chocks is not appropriate. Conversely, having lots of really small wires on a climb with large cracks and mini-chimneys may also not be worth doing. However, do make sure that you have one or two odd-sized bits of gear with you, not just for the unexpected on the route but also for belaying at the top.

Clipping gear onto a harness

You might find it useful to clip gear onto the gear loops upwards rather than downwards. This means that the nose of the karabiner is not pressing onto your body or clothing, and the weight of the rest of the gear on the loop will help it to clip in very smoothly. Most people find this easier than clipping downwards, which can be awkward.

Racking other gear

Slings should be carried neatly around your body (see Chapter 2) so that they are easily accessible and not flapping around. Remember to keep the screwgates open ready for use. A final adjustment could be made to any chocks or rockcentrics on long rope or tape. These tend to swing around, making quite a racket and with the potential of getting tangled around other bits of kit. If you think you are not going to need them for a while clip them up a bit higher by pulling a small loop of rope or tape through the top of the chock, and clipping this into the karabiner. The gear will now be a lot shorter, but can easily be readied for use by letting the small loop drop out of the karabiner and sliding the head of the chock back to the top.

LEADING THE ROUTE

THE FIRST ATTEMPT

Leading your first route is a huge step. Suddenly the stakes are a lot higher and the mind games start to kick in. There is so much more to think about, and simple things get very confusing.

Clients on my courses start by leading far easier routes than they have ever been on before, in a very safe environment with me climbing on a separate top rope alongside. This is so that they can learn how to cope on the 'sharp end' of the rope whilst not having to worry about hanging on for dear life at the same time. After a couple of climbs they will generally have worked out a system for handling everything – racking gear, clipping runners, moving on – and be ready to progress to more challenging routes. It also means that their second, their belayer, will have had a chance to manage the rope and get to grips with using the belay device whilst safeguarding a leader, very different to working on a bottom or top rope.

When I started leading in my mid-teens there was little skill involved (certainly in the way that I was doing it!). Equipment was sparse (my pocket money stretched to buying very little gear) and the meagre rack that a friend and I managed to put together was often used up in the first 10ft of the route! Nowadays many people starting climbing will opt for formal instruction, enabling them to progress safely and steadily through the grades to their own comfort level, using a variety of equipment supplied by the instructor. In this way they can make up their own minds about which direction they wish their climbing to take, as well as providing valuable experience of different styles and makes of technical kit.

So – it's time to start up the route. Everything is sorted and tidied up, all gear selections have been made. Just before you set foot on the rock check once again that you are tied on correctly, and look over at your belayer to make sure that he has you correctly connected to the belay device and is clipped in properly.

It is vital to check each other's set-up every time before starting to climb to ensure the safety of leader and belayer as far as is possible.

9

LEADING

'Diagonal', VS 4c, Huntly's Cave, giving a tricky move around an overhang

There is no need to go through any complicated climbing calls when you are next to each other at the bottom of the route, as these serve to clarify situations when you are at a distance. You might just say 'Climbing', with an 'OK' from your belayer being a sensible response, but as long as he knows you are starting that's enough.

Don't wait too long before thinking about placing your first running belay. You will most likely have spotted a suitable point for this from the ground, but if not start to check the rock for something appropriate after climbing up 1m or so. Once this is in place, you may elect not to put an extender on it, simply to clip the rope in with a spare karabiner. As the runner is so close to the ground extending it any distance will only serve to reduce its effective stopping range. Having a single karabiner in here will also not be a problem as the gear, being so low down, is very unlikely to be dislodged by the movement of the rope. You will also be placing another piece quite soon after it, so clipping straight in will be fine.

Think about the frequency of placements. If your first piece of gear is at 4m the second cannot be more than 3m above that, as the distance you fall plus a bit of rope stretch and the movement of your belayer will mean that you have a high chance of hitting the ground. Mathematically, the higher you climb the wider apart your gear placements could potentially be, in order to stop you hitting the deck. In real life, however, this is far too scary a prospect, and we place runners as and when the opportunity arises.

There are a number of other important factors to consider when leading, and these need to be examined on an individual basis.

Distance to the first runner

As mentioned above, you may have worked out the height of your first running belay before you left the ground. However, the ground immediately underneath the climb also needs to be considered. If it is a flat shingle beach, for example, you may be happy going up for a few moves before placing the first piece, secure in the knowledge that if you do slip the landing is soft. On the other hand, if the terrain were very bouldery or sloping, a slip low down could cause serious injury. In this instance you may even decide to place a piece of gear at head height before leaving the ground, as this will safeguard you for the first couple of moves. Get another piece in as soon as is practicable above it.

Note

It is easy to become very involved in the climbing and end up quite a way above your last runner. This is particularly acute when you are low down, having just left the ground. At this level a single move or two will be enough to take you to a height where you are so far above your protection that a ground fall is a distinct possibility. Bear this in mind when on the lower sections of a climb. It is often easier for your belayer to see what is happening as far as distance is concerned, so take his advice (or ask for it if it is not forthcoming).

Keeping the rope straight

It is important that the climbing rope from the belayer up to you runs in as straight a line as possible. This is for two main reasons.

- Letting a rope zigzag up the climb means that you will be putting a lot of friction into the system. This can get so bad that it becomes almost impossible to pull any slack through as you move up, making things desperate when trying to take in at the top of the crag.
- Having a rope that is not running straight will have a detrimental effect on the runners, which will be pulled sideways and inwards. If the placements are not very good, there is a chance that some will be pulled out, certainly a possibility in the event of a fall.

The proper use of extenders and slings is the answer, and these should be brought into play whenever necessary. Almost all the wires will have an extender on them, but this

9

LEADING

(Left) **Extender being used to bring the rope on a camming device into line**
(Right) **Extender being used to bring the rope line outwards from under a bulge**

could be substituted for a 60cm or even a 120cm sling if they are placed very far off-line. Camming devices are sometimes supplied with a section of sling that can be unwrapped to provide an extension; if this is not enough clip an extender of the appropriate length into the sling. Chocks on wire can also be extended in a similar fashion.

Bear in mind that the rope should not only be straight from left to right, but also needs to be held roughly parallel to the cliff. However, if your route climbs up to a slight bulge, then continues over it and up, and you place a wire under the bulge without extending it enough, you will have the same problems as before: rope drag and a chance of the gear lifting out.

Note

Never clip karabiner to karabiner when extending runners; they could unclip from each other if they end up lying across each other's gates. Always clip a karabiner to software, such as a sling or section of tape.

Holding on to clip gear

Most climbs (when you are learning to lead) will very often have suitable points where you can stop in balance to place gear. Sometimes, however, this may be a little trickier to do, and you will have to hold yourself onto the rock more securely while selecting and placing a runner. This can be quite tiring, especially if you are feeling nervous, in which case you will be holding on tighter and getting more tired – a vicious circle.

Let's say that you have arrived at a point where you want to place a runner, but it is not a particularly easy place to stand, perhaps underneath a bulge that is pushing you out and off balance.

• You have a good hold at shoulder height for your left hand. Select the gear from your harness with your right hand and place it, clipping any surplus kit back onto your gear loops.
• Now swap hands, with your right on the hold where your left was.
• Your left hand can hang down at your side for a few seconds for a rest and a shake out.
• When your left hand has recovered sufficiently, swap hands again and finish off the runner placement with your right. (Obviously your hands may in some cases be the other way round.)

By placing and clipping the gear in this manner you will have given your body the maximum amount of rest, and you should feel better prepared to move on and up the route.

If the runner placement is very tricky, perhaps at the crux move or at a point where you will be off balance, swapping hands might not be enough to give you sufficient rest. Don't be worried about climbing down a little to get a breather before carrying on.

• Climb up to the placement.
• Decide what gear is going to fit, place it and clip it with the rope.
• Downclimb a move or two so that you are back in balance.

After a few moments, when you have got your breath back and are ready to carry on, you can climb up and past the placement.

Note

If you make some type of cunning placement – such as a wire threaded through a gap in some manner – don't forget to tell your second about it. Otherwise he might spend a huge amount of time trying to wiggle it out of a crack when it has just been dropped down from on top.

(Top) **Get the gear ready in plenty of time**

(Bottom) **Getting yourself in balance – here using a shoulder – is useful when placing gear**

Poor gear placements

Although this may sound strange, a poor gear placement can do you some good (see below).

Say you arrive at a point on the route where you want to put in some protection but cannot find anything suitable. You have tried at chest to head height but there is nothing available that you would be really happy with. Try looking lower, even down to feet level. If that is still a blank, have a look to both left and right. If there is still absolutely nothing you have two choices.

- **To move up** and hope for something suitable before long. This may be the more practical but will probably be the most worrying, as you will be getting further away from your last decent piece of gear.
- **To downclimb** a little, still searching for a placement but at least getting nearer the protection of your last runner.

However, if in your searching you come across a possible placement but not a particularly good one, perhaps a 2 (on the scale of 1–5 previously mentioned), it might be worth putting it in and clipping it. It might be a lot better than you thought (conversely, of course, it could be a lot worse!), and it will probably give you more protection than you have had for the last couple of metres (which may be none). What it might do, though, is to give you the confidence to step up a move or two and get a really good piece into a crack that is just out of reach.

This so-called 'psychological protection' should not be placed or used lightly. Its main purpose is to help you to relax so that you can make that extra move. However, I would only suggest using it if the piece of gear below is not only not very far away but also bombproof (4 or 5). It may, though, give you the necessary boost to climb higher, clip better gear and complete the route in style.

TIRED ARMS, TIRED BODY

You can get tired at any point during the climb, not just when placing protection. One of the problems, as mentioned above, is that the more tired you get the more worried you become – so the harder you hang on and the more tired you get – and it is hard to break the pattern.

Mental preparation is important; having an attitude that you will succeed usually means that you will. However, leaders do get tired, and it is important to be aware of the signs that things aren't going too well.

Sewing machine leg Also known as 'disco leg' (or the very descriptive 'doing an Elvis') this is really linked to nervousness, exacerbated by awkward body positioning. You get a bit tired and off balance, and one of your legs (in extreme cases it could be both) starts to vibrate of its own accord. This is extremely off-putting and potentially quite a problem, as should the foot of the vibrating leg be on a small hold it could wobble itself off quite quickly.

It can be cured, and experienced climbers rarely suffer from it. They will have learnt to control their fear in different situations, and will also have the skills to shift their position slightly when stationary, which makes all the difference. So what can you do about it?

Tip

A nut key is an essential piece of gear, and is usually carried by the second. However, on routes that are a bit dirty, on multi-pitch climbs and in mountains, it would be worth carrying one when leading. When faced with a crack that is choked up with mud, grass and debris you can do a bit of excavation and possibly unearth that perfect (and previously hidden) placement. It also makes placing slings through threads a lot easier, as the hook end of the key can be pushed through, a loop of the sling hooked and then pulled through.

9

LEADING

- Relax (tricky if you are hanging on for dear life some way above your last piece of protection) – it will definitely help. Relaxing lessens the tension in muscles, often the underlying cause of a vibrating leg. Think about how good the holds are, how safe you really are and how nothing can go wrong. A few deep breaths will also help.
- Move your position slightly. This will shift the load point under your foot to a different area, and will also mean that the rest of the leg muscles are being used in a different manner, which should ease the problem.
- If that still doesn't solve it, downclimb a little until you are well in balance, take a few moments to compose yourself, and then carry back on up.

Being 'pumped' Your arms can get quite tired, and this is often a feeling described as 'being pumped'. This is particularly noticeable in the forearms, and results from the build-up of lactic acid due to your arms being worked at above shoulder height for a period of time. This can creep in really quickly, sometimes after only a couple of moves, so you need to know how to deal with it. One of the main causes is, yet again, nerves, as the more scared you are the tighter you hang on so the more pumped you get. Once again relaxing is the first line of defence, although this will not go all the way to solving it.

This affects even top climbers – no one is immune. Many climbers use a climbing wall or bouldering circuit to train their bodies to beat the problem. They will traverse and climb as much as possible until they become really pumped, step off and have a recovery period. They will then repeat the process. By so doing they build up a lactic tolerance, their body knows what to expect when working at extremes and so becomes more able to cope with it. Also, when on a climb they will have a way of holding on that allows them to take a rest with the opportunity to 'shake out'. The climber, getting a bit pumped, hangs on with one hand and drops the other down by his side, giving a bit of a shake so that the lactic acid build-up decreases and the blood returns, rejuvenating the arm muscles.

Although it may take a number of years to build up a high lactic tolerance, we can certainly shake out and recover in that way. Being in balance will make a lot of difference.

- If you are starting to feel a bit 'pumped' spend a minute on a suitable ledge; drop each arm in turn down by your side for a few moments and give it a gentle shake.

- If you are on a tricky bit of the route and feel you are getting pumped, do the same as when placing gear. Hold onto a suitably friendly piece of the rock, drop one arm down and shake it out. Now swap hands and do the same for the other arm. This should give you enough recovery to carry on up and over the obstacle.

Remember that it is less tiring to hang on a straight arm than on a bent one. This is because most of the load will be on bone rather than on muscle. If you need to rest an arm for a moment, find a suitable hold some distance away and keep the supporting arm straight. Alternatively, if the good hold is low down, bend your knees so that the arm is straight and the other can be dropped low to rest for a while.

Relax where possible, letting your feet take the weight, and rest your arms for a moment. Climbing at Gorbio, southern France, on 'Les Restanques', Grade 4.

FALLING OFF

This is something that we don't plan for, yet it could happen at any time. Climbers pushing the limits at the top end of the sport take falling off as part of the deal, and as mentioned above they are mentally prepared for it. After you have tried it a few times at the climbing wall you will know what to expect, but it is still a shock when it happens for real.

It is very unusual to fall off without knowing it is about to happen. Making a move where your foot shoots off a wet hold, for instance, or pulling on a small handhold that snaps off may be totally unexpected, but usually you will know in advance that you may take a bit of a flight. Warn your belayer: although he should be ready for anything it would be comforting to know that he is braced and prepared. If possible, climb down a little towards your last runner so that you if you do fall you won't travel any distance. Make sure that you have not stepped inside the rope (see below) and that nothing is going to catch on the way down. Try to maintain as square a posture as possible and (although this may sound impossible) relax. Being tense is a sure way to hurt yourself, not least because you may be tempted to grab hold of something as you go, perhaps injuring your hand or arm, or even turning you upside down.

A FIRST FALL

Falling? It all seems very easy, at least on the big screen. The climber tries a move and, having missed the crucial hold, drops from the cliff to end up some 30ft lower down, smiling and suspended by a thin length of taught nylon. It all seems very easy – they don't even scream.

Why is it, then, that I am now absolutely, utterly terrified? The answer is that I think that I'm about to fall off. This is one of my first leads, and my cockiness has led me to the Roaches in Staffordshire to try a tricky climb, one that looks fairly straightforward from the guidebook description. It isn't – at least not to me.

A massive 2ft above my last piece of protection I can neither advance nor retreat, and my right leg has started involuntarily to vibrate up and down. The piece of protection that I recently placed now looks pathetic. Far from being the '5' rating I gave it initially, my mind now assesses it as a ' minus 5', seeing that there is a chance that I will soon be testing it out for real. Also, I am now convinced that the knot securing the rope to my harness has miraculously untied itself during the last two minutes, sentencing me to an unhindered flight to the jagged boulders far below.

Of course, none of the above is actually for real. I'm about to take my first proper leader fall and my mind is starting to play tricks. Why can't I be as mellow as the heroes that I've seen in the films? It's because this is new to me, unknown ground, and even though I've read up on the subject I have absolutely no idea what is going to happen.

I'm going to find out soon enough. My hands are sweating and a futile attempt to downclimb only results in a short slip. I briefly stop myself with one ▶

◄ hand on a sloping hold until I can grip no longer – and down I go. The scream, I believe, could have been heard somewhere near the English Channel. Then, suddenly, I stop. Something's wrong: no snapping of bones on boulders, no ambulance, no helicopter – not even the sound of the holy choir invisible. Just me hanging there, a couple of feet below my last piece of gear, unharmed, with life going on around me as if nothing had happened.

My runner had indeed been as good as I had thought when placing it. No knots had come undone, nothing had snapped, pulled out or even been strained. Everything had worked exactly as I had been told it would.

So what can we learn from this episode? The main thing is to be prepared and to not fear what you know to be a safe event – falling onto a well-placed piece of gear with a good belayer with no other element in the system that can fail. Following on from this traumatic experience early on in my climbing career, I decided that falling could be a safe activity; the mystery – and hence the fear – had gone. I was therefore able to push my climbing grade higher and higher, confident in the knowledge that if I did fail and take to the air, providing I had all the necessary back-ups in place it would be little more than an annoying inconvenience.

Thus, from that day on, I happily fell from climbs the world over. I even managed to get up a few.

BEING LOWERED OFF

This will not happen very often, as a climb will normally top-out and you will walk down or sometimes abseil off. However, if you are off route, the climb is too hard, the weather or darkness are closing in, for example, you may elect to descend from where you are. This may just be a short distance to a ledge where you can have a rest and then try again, hopefully successfully, but if this is not an option you will have to go all the way down.

There is an extremely important consideration when you, as a leader, are thinking about being lowered off. Your highest piece of gear, through which the rope will be running, will be taking the entire load: not just your weight but most of your belayer's – who is counterbalancing you during the descent – as well. If you and your belayer both weigh 75kg the top runner will be taking a load of near

Atmospheric climbing on unusual rock – the top of 'Python Cracks Direct', VS 4c, on Clach na Beinn, Scotland

enough 150kg. This load will not be constant. The worst-case scenario would be when you descend a bit fast and your belayer puts on the brakes; the load will increase by roughly twice your bodyweight as your weight comes onto the rope (see Appendix 1).

If the last placement was ideal – say a 5 – there should be no problem. If less than that there is a chance it could fail. You could back it up; another piece of gear placed alongside it might make all the difference and allow you to descend in safety. On the other hand, you may be going down because you are off route, or the climb is just horrible and not worth doing, and the runner in front of you is the only one that you can find. In this case the best answer is to downclimb, taking as much weight off the rope as possible. Your second can keep the rope snug but it must run smoothly and not be jerked. If you descend a short distance and spot a better runner placement, it may be worth putting a bit of gear in and clipping this into the rope as a back-up.

Once you are down, your second may wish to become leader and have a go. If not, you will either have to retrieve your kit after pulling the rope down, or abandon it. Retrieval is best done by abseil (see Chapter 11), looking after your own security at all times. If this is not possible then you will have no option but to leave the gear behind. If so (and you have thought this through prior to being lowered) you will probably have stripped out all the lower pieces of protection as you came down. You are only likely to lose a minimal amount of gear, but don't scrimp – if you need to leave more than one piece in place to protect yourself during the descent then do so. It's better to lose a bit of gear than to lose your life.

HAVING A LONG RUN-OUT

The run-out is the distance between you as leader and your last piece of protection. Most of us will opt for a short run-out, as getting too far above your gear is too scary! However, sometimes a long run-out may be unavoidable, often because the gear placements aren't as frequent as you may like, necessitating you to move higher and higher in search of a good bit of gear. Having a good look from the bottom of the route may help to avoid this; if the line of the climb seems devoid of placements you could decide to go somewhere else. Guidebooks sometimes give information about the amount of gear, and apart from the make-up of the grade (see Chapter 1) some terminology may help. A route may be described as 'hard to protect' or as having 'infrequent runners' or, more esoterically, a phrase such as 'make a bold move up' should give you a clue.

9

LEADING

If you find yourself in the situation of having no gear, with little obvious prospect of some appearing in the near future, the most sensible option is to downclimb. You can then take stock from a position closer to your last runner. Perhaps you are off route, maybe you missed a good placement on the way up, or perhaps there just aren't any. If in any doubt no one will blame you for calling it quits and downclimbing, taking your gear out as you go.

Another time when you may be tempted to voluntarily have a long run-out is where the ground becomes very easy. This is quite common on multi-pitch and mountain routes, where the meaty part of the climbing has been completed and all that remains is to romp to the top. Be very careful, however, because even though you may be happy on the easier ground there will always be a loose hold or a patch of slippery moss waiting to catch you out. If you are some distance above your last piece of gear you will certainly take a long fall.

The last climb of the day

RUN RABBIT...

A number of years ago I was nearly killed by a rabbit. I was on a long route on the Scottish coast, only single pitch but a full rope length. The hard bit was all low down, so from about midway it was an easy romp to the top. Being very confident I just carried on climbing, enjoying the easy ground and not thinking about the huge run-out I was getting into. Just as I poked my head over the top edge of the cliff, a rabbit leapt out of its hole right in front of my face. It startled me so much that I jumped – both my feet came off their holds, and it was only because I had good handholds that I didn't fall back down the route. If I had done so, so long was my run-out that I would certainly have hit the ledge just above the sea. Thus, whenever I feel that clients on a climbing course are maybe a bit far above their protection I remind them about the killer rabbit and they know what I mean. Worth remembering.

COMMUNICATION

Careful and competent communication between you and your belayer is really important. Unless you are both completely happy and relaxed you may get very involved in the job in hand and neglect your belayer, who is as much a part of the climb as you are. Tell him what is going on, what gear is good, about a particularly good hold, and so on. If you need to call out any technical requirements, such as 'Slack' or 'Take in', keep to the 'official' form to avoid confusion.

AT THE TOP

You've done the route and reached the top. You've got that elated feeling (the reason why most people climb). However, the job is not over and there are a couple of things that you need to do, not least bringing up your second.

Bearing in mind the comments made in Chapter 5 (Climbing Calls) about being 'safe', make a judgement about how you feel. Always err on the side of caution and get yourself anchored (unless you are absolutely sure that you are in no danger). Choose a suitable point to belay from and make sure that you are reasonably comfortable, near enough the edge so that you can communicate and hopefully see your second for at least part of the way up, but not so close that you are in danger of being pulled over the edge should he slip. Give the appropriate series of climbing calls and, with him on belay, bring him up.

Bringing up your second

Belaying a second can be, in the nicest possible way, a bit like trying to land a fish! You are constantly feeling for him on the rope, pulling in a little until you feel his bodyweight, waiting until he moves off again and taking in some more. Don't pull the rope too hard (unless he asks you to do so), as you will affect how he is climbing. Just feel him on the end and no more, perhaps even slackening off a tiny bit. Make sure that the dead rope is away from where he is going to exit and not hanging down the cliff where it could get snagged.

Removing gear

There is a chance that your second may have a little difficulty retrieving a runner that you have placed, especially if you have loaded it at all. He may have to get both hands to it, which will probably mean that he needs you to take his weight on the rope. He will need to move up slightly so that when he weights the system the rope stretch takes him to the correct point, and may need to move up once or twice and sag back onto it as the system settles.

If this is taking a long time it may be a better idea to retrieve the gear by abseil. This is particularly true of camming devices, as a bit of thought and time may need to go into removing them.

Once your second arrives at the top, keep him on belay until he has moved a little way back from the edge and stated that he is 'Safe'. Take him off the belay device, let him know that you have done so, sort the gear out and go and do another route!

COMMON ERRORS

Stepping under the rope

This happens quite frequently. Most of the time it is not a problem, but if you are in a situation where there is a chance that you are going to fall off it can become a serious issue. If you have a foot on the inside of the rope above a runner, should you fall your foot will slide down and get stuck above the piece of gear. Even if this is only momentary, it will be enough to flip you upside down, possibly causing severe back and head injury. If you need to step one foot to the other side of the rope make sure that it is placed around the outside. If you then fall your foot has no chance of becoming trapped.

Back-clipping

This is a very common error that, at first glance, does not appear to be too serious. However, a karabiner that is back-clipped has the potential to undo under load.

When you clip your rope into an extender or piece of gear, it should run from your belayer, go in at the back end of the karabiner and come out from the front, passing across the back bar. As you move on and upwards the karabiner will sit in the correct orientation.

In back-clipping the rope runs from your belayer, in through the front of the karabiner on the runner, then out from the back to your harness. As you move past the karabiner will tend to rotate horizontally by 180°. This can cause problems:

- If the placement is not particularly good, perhaps a wire poorly placed in a shallow pocket, the rotating movement of the karabiner on the extender can be such that it displaces the wire from its crack.
- Much more important is the way that the rope can end up running across the karabiner's gate. If this happens there is a chance of the rope unclipping itself as you move upwards, simply by the pressure of the rope pressing on the gate.
- In a fall situation there is a chance that the rope will run across the gate and unclip when it is loaded – the load being your bodyweight coming onto it. This will obviously be catastrophic, and every effort should be made to prevent this from happening.

(Left) **Placing your foot underneath the rope can cause you to flip upside down in the event of a fall**

(Right) **Keeping your foot outside the rope ensures that any fall will not be hindered by it getting trapped**

(Above) **Karabiner back-clipped**

(Below) **Karabiner clipped correctly**

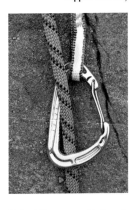

(Below) **Two runners Z-clipped**

Clipping the karabiner the right way first time, so that it hangs in the correct orientation, is the best form of insurance. Rotating the karabiner in the extender will also help to solve the problem in some cases.

Snap karabiners with bentgates, designed to facilitate the easy clipping in of a rope, also work in reverse, with easy clipping out also being a feature. Take extra care that the rope is being placed correctly. If you are using slings to extend the runner into line you may elect to just use straight-gate snap karabiners on them; even if they have been clipped correctly it only takes a small amount of rotation to move the gate into the firing line of the rope.

Z-clipping

This can happen when nerves get the better of a leader and he clips runners in the wrong order, only possible if the runners are very close to each other, such as below a crux sequence on a tricky climb. Z-clipping is where the rope has been taken from below the last runner and clipped into the karabiner on the one that has just been placed. This results in the rope running from the belayer, up to the top runner, down to the one just below, then back up to the leader. As the leader moves on and up a lot of drag will be put into the system, perhaps so much that he can't move. It also means that he is not protected by the top runner but still by the lower one, thus facing a longer fall should he slip.

To remedy this, unclip the rope from the lower of the two runners. It will now be on the top one, and the lower one can be clipped back in at its proper position, just underneath.

This often happens when you are suffering from nerves, and placing a couple of pieces of gear will help to steady them. When feeling a bit twitchy you may pull yourself closer into the rock whilst clipping, accidentally making a Z-clip.

Note

For these problems – stepping through, back-clipping and Z-clipping – your belayer will often be in a better position than you to see what is going on. A good second will spot these potential problems and let you know about them. It would be sensible to act upon this advice straight away before the problem worsens.

A FIRST VS LEAD

My first Very Severe lead took place at Swanage, my local stamping ground, with Botany Bay, VS 4c being the route of choice. The long-suffering Simon was my partner and our rack consisted of a few wires, a couple of large 'stoppers' on rope and three slings. I was to lead the route, so I set off, only to find that the crux move, the very hardest part, was right near the bottom. I managed to place a reasonable piece of protection but ended up getting very tired because of hanging on, and just had enough energy to climb back down to the narrow ledge perched above the sea. I gave the rack to Simon and he had a go, getting no higher than I had. Also becoming very tired from hanging onto the lower section he came back down as well.

I had recovered by now, so I took the rack back and had another go. Still no good: the move through the crux was not giving up easily. Simon then tried again, then me, then him and then finally, on about my fifth go, I cracked it. I pulled through the crux and onto a small ledge above, extremely pleased but with very tired arms. Elation, however, was short-lived. It dawned on me that we had been so intent on overcoming the problem of the first section of the route that I had completely forgotten to take the rack from Simon prior to my triumphant final attempt.

I was now halfway up a VS, the first I had ever led, a long way above the sea and not an inconsiderable distance above the last runner. With the options of downclimbing or lowering a loop of rope to bring up the spare gear either impossible or impractical, I had no choice but to solo up the rest of the route. I arrived, gibbering and not a little sweaty, onto the top of the cliff, and lay there for some minutes in order to get my pulse rate and breathing back down to normal.

The main lesson learned was that you should always take a moment before starting to climb to check that all your gear is in order, and that nothing has been left behind. Run through a mental process and tick off the kit that you need, and check that it is all arranged in the appropriate manner. After that there's just the climbing to contend with!

9

LEADING

10 SECONDING A CLIMB

Seconding a climb may seem like the easy job, but in many respects it's harder to get right than leading. All the leader has to do is wander up a piece of rock and place protection at various intervals. This may be over-simplifying things – and he does risk falling off – but as far as actual workload is concerned he has an easy time of it. When seconding a climb, however, there is a lot to do: rope management, belaying, paying out and taking in, watching for problems, spotting, being ready to hold a fall, advising on the direction to take as well as giving advice about runners are a few of the more important tasks. All of this whilst standing – possibly lashed down to an anchor – at the bottom of a draughty crag with your head tilted back at 90°, answering questions from passers-by whilst their dog sniffs your leg!

Having a second in whom you can trust is a huge part of getting your head around the whole psychology of climbing. It is amazing how many people climb without really trusting their belayer, which will have a detrimental effect on how they move over rock. Trusting your second gives you one less thing to worry about; you can devote all your effort into leading the route knowing that you will be as safe as possible in his hands.

This chapter covers the various skills needed by a second. Getting all this right will only be achieved through practice, but it won't take long to get into a routine and it'll soon become second nature.

MANAGING THE ROPE
This – along with belaying – is a very important skill. It is very easy for anyone to dump the rope on the ground and tie onto the end, but doing it in a manner that ensures the rope is as hassle-free as possible takes a bit of thought.

Consider where you are going to be to belay. This will normally be close into the base of the climb, so look for somewhere you can stand on level ground. You may decide to set up ground anchors, and if so this will usually dictate where you end up in relation to the bottom of the route.

Once you have decided on your position, uncoil the rope. Run it through, checking that there are no kinks or twists, onto your correct side; if you are going to operate the belay device with your right hand the rope needs to be on your right-hand side. Conversely, if you are going to operate it with your left hand, place the rope on the left-hand side. Don't be tempted to put the rope down and then drag it into position, as this is guaranteed to end up with knots.

When uncoiling the rope (or rather unflaking it – see Chapter 2) start by laying one end off where it will not be covered by the remainder. Run it through your hands right to the other end. The leader will tie onto this end – the one coming out of the top of the pile – while the belayer will tie onto the other end, underneath the pile.

Always be alert to what the leader is doing – it's your turn next! 'Gangway', Severe 4a.

SECONDING A CLIMB

GROUND ANCHORS

This is a method by which the belayer ties himself down at the bottom of the route, to provide enhanced security for both him and the leader. Whether or not to use ground anchors will rely on a number of factors:

- Provision of anchor points.
- Weight difference between leader and belayer.
- Number of runners likely to be on the route.
- Ground around the belayer (flat or, for example, a small ledge above the sea).

Provision of anchor points

In an ideal world there will be one anchor behind you at ground level, and possibly another at around shoulder height in front. The first will stop you from being pulled forward and upward in the event of a fall, the second one will keep you from slipping or tripping over with the possible consequence of pulling the leader off. A third option, one low down in front, will also go a long way to providing security.

Weight differential

This may be a crucial factor in deciding whether or not to anchor at the bottom. If the belayer is heavier than the leader you may choose to do without. However, if the leader is the heavier it would be wise to anchor the belayer.

Having a heavier belayer than leader is not, of course, reason to do without ground anchors in every situation. There may be issues with the ground at the base of the climb being uneven, or a lack of runners on the route meaning that the leader will take a substantial length of fall, thus a subsequent loading on the system, should he come off.

Runners on the route

If there are a lot of runner placements available on the climb, the weight of a falling leader will have a lesser impact on the belayer than if the gear was sparsely placed, so giving him more time to accelerate on the way down. Also, if the runners are not as good as they could be, the belayer not being tied down will help the leader. It has been shown that a belayer moving 1m upwards when holding a fall massively reduces the shock-loading and impact force on runners, which may make the difference between them holding or being pulled out.

Surrounding ground

This may be a deciding factor when thinking about whether or not to use a ground anchor. If the terrain at the bottom of the route is quite flat, and you are happy with other issues (difference in weight and the provision of frequent and good runners) you may decide to not tie yourself down. However, if you were belaying on a ledge above the sea, for instance, or on a multi-pitch climb, tying yourself at least onto the rock in front of you would be sensible.

Consider also the single-pitch climb with bouldery ground at the bottom. Being pulled along when holding a fall, subsequently tripping over a boulder and being dragged forwards, possibly letting go of the rope, is a real possibility. So too is the not-uncommon scenario in which the belayer moves position slightly, perhaps to see the leader better, trips over and pulls him off the climb.

Using ground anchors
It is possible to clip straight into a ground anchor with a sling, although this is not ideal. A sling is made from a non-stretch material and will not work as a shock absorber. A far better method is to tie in with the rope using a normal combination of clove hitch or figure of eight knots, adjusted as required.

(Top left) **Tied onto a ground anchor from behind**

(Top right) **Tied onto a ground anchor from behind and high in front**

(Bottom left) **Ground anchor coming from low down in front**

(Bottom right) **Good, braced position when using a ground anchor**

BELAYING POSITION

This is an essential element of correct belaying, but one that is often overlooked.

It is important that the rope runs in a straight line up the route via the runners, so that in the event of a fall they are all loaded correctly. To ensure this the belayer must be close into the bottom of the climb. It is very tempting, especially when trying to watch what is going on, to step back a distance. By this action the belayer alters the angle at which the rope runs up through the gear, increasing the chance of it lifting out when loaded.

Imagine the rope running from the leader, through the runners to the bottom one and then to your belay device. If the rope is loaded, such as in a fall, it will come tight with the leader's weight being held by the top runner. The bottom runner will then bisect the angle made by the rope. If you are standing any distance away it will be pulled in an upwards direction, possibly causing it to pull out. Once that has happened the second piece of gear will be affected in the same way, possibly also failing. All subsequent runners will also be affected; if they come out

(Top left) **Standing too far out with protection lifting**

(Bottom left) **Standing in a correct position, with gear hanging correctly**

(Right) **Very poor belaying: the leader will hit the ground if he falls, even if his runners do manage to stay in**

Rope

Belayer

and the top runner fails under the leader's bodyweight he will fall to the ground.

There are two ways of ensuring this cannot happen:

- Make sure that you are belaying close into the base of the route. The rope will then run in a straight line and the runners will hang as intended.
- If it is not possible for you to be close in, the first runner, even very low down, can be placed as a directional runner to direct the rope up the line of the climb, with the result that none of the others will be pulled outwards.

Note

Be very careful if using a low-down directional runner. The direction of pull on you as belayer will be completely different, and it is very hard holding a fall when the loading comes from straight in front of you. In this case, a ground anchor from behind would be a sensible aid to stop you being pulled off your feet in the event of a leader fall.

SPOTTING

This is the process by which the belayer provides a bit of security to the leader for the initial few moves of a climb, before the first piece of gear is placed. If the leader slipped off after the first couple of metres he could turn an ankle or fall backwards and sustain an even worse injury, especially on uneven ground. Spotting allows you to 'guide' him down should he slip, helping him to keep his body upright and to reduce the loading on his knees and ankles.

Take up a braced position behind the leader, arms outstretched and one leg behind the other in a strong 'V' shape. If he slips you don't catch him and lower him down – that would be almost impossible – but guide him down to a safe landing and stop him staggering backwards and tripping over. Look out for your own safety at the same time, and ensure that your footing is stable. Spotting is not always necessary but can make for a happy leader at the start of some routes.

WATCHING FOR PROBLEMS

You will be in a very good position at the bottom of the climb to spot any potential problems. You will notice Z-clipping, stepping through, zigzagging and back-clipping (see Chapter

10

Tip

Pay out enough rope prior to spotting so that the leader can climb without being tugged, and be ready to take in as soon as he has clipped into the first runner.

Note

There is a limit to how effective spotting can be. If the leader is well above arm's reach and still wants to be spotted he is on the wrong route. Also, should he slip from this height he could injure the belayer. Get him to come down and choose a climb where the start is protected by a runner lower down.

Bear in mind that
although a hold may
look superb from
below it may be useless
when looked at from a
practical sense. Also, if
a hold looks obvious to
you but the leader
ignores it, it may be
hard to appreciate why.
Think about it from the
leader's point of view:
using it may put him
totally out of balance,
or may require him to
let go with the only
hand or foot that's
keeping him in contact
with the rock!

Tip

Unless the leader is in a
chatty mood, keep con-
versation clear and con-
cise. He is probably
very busy with the job
in hand and concentrat-
ing hard, and doesn't
want to know about a
particular bird that has
just landed close by! If
there is a lot of ambient
noise lengthy instruc-
tions can be hard to
hear and interpret, caus-
ing confusion.

9) before the leader who will be absorbed in a world of his own. When belaying you can see the bigger picture, particularly what is happening below the leader's feet, and advise him accordingly. You may also be able to see holds that he is missing, and advise on the route direction.

Attentive belaying, looking out for any problems

PAYING OUT THE ROPE

This is a particularly tricky skill to master. I often liken it to playing a fish on a line, constantly adjusting by taking in and paying out, making sure the tension is just right and that the rope is not too slack. It is important that the leader can move unhindered by the rope, but is never in any danger, if he falls off, of travelling any great distance because the rope was slack. The belayer should have one hand on the dead rope and the other on the live, feeding it in and out of the belay device as needed.

When the leader is clipping a runner above his head, he will reach down and pull a metre or two of rope through. Anticipate this and be ready to pay it out. With the runner clipped he will climb up, needing you to take in, and as he passes the runner he will need more rope, so you pay out again. Belaying involves constantly taking in and paying out, without ever tugging on the leader or having reams of rope drooping down in front of your belay device.

HOLDING A FALL

This is where you earn your money! At some stage in your climbing career you will probably have to hold your first leader fall. Hopefully this will just be a short slump onto a piece of handy gear, but it could be a large 'lob' for quite a distance above a runner, causing consternation all around! The outcome of both of these falls should be the same; the leader brushes himself off and starts back up the route again, ego dented but otherwise none the worse for wear.

Holding a fall – or more specifically the thought of having to hold one – is a very scary prospect. However, as long as everything is in place (runners, the line the rope takes and your ability to hold onto the dead rope) it will be over in an instant and you'll wonder what all the fuss was about. You will almost certainly get some warning that the leader is about to come off, as he will usually be aware that it is going to happen. Even if he is trying a hard move and doesn't intend to fall, he will at least have made you aware that it is a possibility. At the higher levels of climbing taking falls is an accepted fact, with some climbers taking many falls onto the same piece of gear as they try to work out a particular sequence.

- **Look out for your own security**. If you think a fall is imminent, get yourself into a braced position and, if a ground anchor is not being used get close into the bottom of the route. This will ensure that you hold an upwards pull, not an outwards one. A foot out against the rock will help to keep you in balance.

Note

Use both hands when feeding the rope out to the leader as he climbs, one on the live rope and one on the dead. Simply allowing him to tug it out of the belay device for himself as he ascends will make it very hard for him to progress and can cause problems when clipping runners.

10

SECONDING A CLIMB

Note

Make sure that, in the event of a fall, you cannot be pulled forwards and injure yourself on a projecting rock or tree. Don't stand directly underneath the leader; if he falls further than intended he could land on you.

Note

Ropes are very strong and designed to safely hold a number of long falls. However, if a fall is significant, you should check the rope for damage, particularly if there is a chance that it has been running over a sharp edge. If you are in any doubt, return the rope to whoever you bought it from, or if this is not possible contact the manufacturer via their web site, as they are usually very helpful. If there is still any doubt in your mind, replacing the rope will be far better than risking the consequences of using one that is damaged.

- **As the leader is about to come off** he'll yell something like 'Take', and then fall. The belayer holds on tight to the rope and lets its elasticity do the job of reducing the shock-loading on runners. This is where the belayer's 1m of lift (mentioned earlier in this chapter) comes into play, as it allows an even greater reduction in shock-loading throughout the system.

- **Carefully take in any slack rope** between the two of you, but don't take it in so tight as to pull him off. Often, a leader may think that he is about to come off but somehow regains his balance and composure and stays on the rock. Tugging him at this point will be disastrous, not only for him but also for your ongoing friendship!

- **Give the leader a moment to compose himself** after a fall. Don't be too quick to lower him straight down to the ground, as he may want to get back onto the rock and try again. Let him stay and rest for a minute before continuing or deciding to descend.

LOWERING THE LEADER

It is possible that the leader will need to be lowered off at some stage. This can happen for a number of reasons: the route being too hard, daylight running out or weather conditions changing. If the leader is to come down what happens next? He may just want to be lowered down to a ledge from where he can have a rest and try the section again. Hopefully he will be successful this time and the climb can continue as normal. If not, however, he may want to be lowered to the ground and call it a day. Perhaps you want to have a go at leading the route yourself. If not the rope will have to be pulled down and you both move on to somewhere else.

A belayer holding the leader during the lower needs to be in as balanced and braced a position as possible. This will normally be at the bottom of the crag, perhaps with one foot up against it or a suitable rock for increased stability. Both hands are on the dead rope, which should be fed through slowly and smoothly – the leader will soon let you know if you are going too fast. A ground anchor will be useful, especially if the leader is heavier than you. If you do not have one in place already it would not be practical to construct one just prior to lowering.

FOLLOWING THE CLIMB

Once the leader reaches the top of the route and shouts down that he is safe (see Chapter 5), and you have taken him off your belay device, you can get ready to climb.

On a multi-pitch route, or one where you are standing on a small ledge above the sea, for instance, you would not disconnect any of your anchor system until you hear 'Climb when you are ready'. It is only after that point that you are on belay and safe to take out the gear.

However, on a single-pitch crag with a safe area from which you are belaying you can start getting things ready straight away. Dismantle any ground anchors and retrieve all the gear, either taking it with you or putting it away in your rucksack, if it is close by. When the leader shouts 'Taking in', get yourself to the bottom of the route so that all the slack rope can be pulled up. Remember to keep the calls concise and clear, as it may be tricky hearing each other and you don't want any confusion to arise. After hearing 'OK', you can start up the route.

Try to remember where the leader went, and the positions of the most useful hand- and footholds. Also make a note of any unusually placed gear he told you about so that you don't have to spend a long time trying to work it out.

RETRIEVING GEAR

This can sometimes be more difficult than placing gear, especially where, for example, the leader gave a nut a good tug to seat it properly. Lifting out gear will usually best be done from the position it was put in, so think ahead and decide where the leader was placed. There will probably be a ledge or good holds at that point. Most gear will have been placed at chest to head height, so don't be tempted to climb past any and then have to perform gymnastics to reach down and retrieve it. Climbing past not only means that you end up in a lead situation, it will also very likely cause the placement to invert, possibly jamming it in tighter.

Wires

When removing a wire, stop at a comfortable point and have a quick look to see how it was placed. Keeping it clipped to the rope, grasp the wire as close to the rock as possible and gently lift it up, maintaining the same orientation as when it was placed. A push on the head of the nut or a slight wiggle can help. Once it is out, let it hang so that you can unclip the extender from the rope. The wire and extender can now be clipped to a gear loop on your harness, best done with the karabiner that connects the two parts together so that it only hangs down a short distance. If you clipped the karabiner at the end of the extender into a gear loop the wire would hang down by your knees with a chance of it catching as you continued on and up.

10

SECONDING A CLIMB

(Above left) **Hold the wire as close to the rock as possible**
(Above right) **Clip the wire to your harness using the central karabiner**

(Below) **Retrieve a cam from below, and be careful not to invert it**

Large chocks

As large chocks, such as rockcentrics, often have a much bigger head than wires, it is often possible to get your hand into the crack where they were placed and wiggle them out. They may need to be rotated slightly to reduce the camming action before releasing, but due to their large surface contact area this is usually easily done. The most stubborn will need a tap with the nut key to get them moving.

Camming devices

These should be treated with respect. If you move them incorrectly they can 'walk' into the back of the crack or shift slightly and open up a cam, making them irretrievable. Stop below the cam if possible, and don't let the rope pull tight on the karabiner (which can make them shift position). Most cams have a hypodermic syringe-type mechanism, usually involving your thumb being on the end of the shaft section with a finger or two hooked onto the release bar or trigger. The shaft will need to be pushed in very slightly so that the cams can be retracted before taking it out. Once retrieved, clip it to your gear loop so that it hangs down as little as possible. As for the wires, if it has an extender on it then clip it to yourself using the middle karabiner to keep it out of the way.

If the cam has walked into the crack, the hook on the end of the nut key can be used instead of your fingers to reach into the trigger mechanism. The smaller sizes may have been rigged with a pull cord connecting the trigger to the end of the central bar (see Chapter 2), in which case pulling on this should solve the problem.

Slings

These should be removed with great care. Those over spikes present little problem, but any that are threaded should not be tugged hard, otherwise they could jam in the crack and be impossible to remove. Once the sling is off, wrap it over your arm and across the chest in its original position for secure carrying.

Tip

When removing a sling from an awkward thread, use your nut key. This can be pushed into the gap and used to steer the sling around the bend, helping to avoid it getting stuck.

Using a nut key

This requires a little bit of skill. Although a very simple piece of kit, incorrect use could damage the wire for good. Don't jab at the nut, as you could damage the wire fibres. Slide the head of the key along the wire until its heel sits on the head of the nut at the point where the wires emerge. A sharp push should be enough to dislodge the gear. If not, try again. If after a couple of tries this still does not work get both hands free (you may need to be taken in tight), hold the key in place with one hand and hit the end of it with the heel of the other.

Note

Do not be tempted to grasp the extender and use it to tug the wire sharply upwards to retrieve it. This will often rotate the head and jam it in tighter. The point where the wire enters the head of the nut will be stressed, causing a deformation of the metal fibres that make up the wire. This weakens it considerably, and a wire with an angled head should be discarded.

SECONDING A CLIMB

Tip

If you know that a piece of gear has been wedged in – perhaps a wire that has been fallen on – you could take a 'secret weapon' up with you: a handy piece of rock from the base of the cliff. You are unlikely to be able to push the wire out using just the nut key, as it will probably be tightly wedged. Have your belayer keep you on a tight rope so that you can use both hands, and place the heel of the nut key on the head of the nut, just by where the wire enters. Now tap the end of the nut key smartly with the rock, and the wire should be released. Take great care not to drop the rock when carrying it up or using it. Dispose of it safely by dropping it to the ground when there is no one nearby, rather than carting it up the rest of the route.

Tapping the end of the nut key should help release problem wires

Tip

If working hard to get out a wire that is well stuck, keep your face out of the way. If it suddenly releases it could hit you in the face.

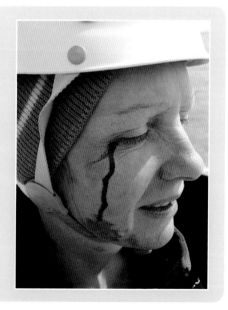

Keep your head out of the way when pulling out gear!

GETTING TO THE TOP

So that's it: the climb completed. Once you have finished and climbed up over the edge, walk back a little way and say 'Safe' to your belayer, so he knows that he can relax and take you off his device. You can now untie and help get the rope coiled up. Be very careful, though, before helpfully unclipping your partner from the anchor. He may be leaning out to take a photograph or for a better view down the crag, and if you have taken him off the anchor he could fall over the edge – it certainly wouldn't be the first time that's happened. Always check with him that he has finished with the system before undoing anything.

It is worth sorting the gear out at this stage, so unclip it from your gear loops and lay it out on a suitable piece of rock or ground, so that your partner can clip it all back into place on his harness. This also serves as a check that you did retrieve all of it, and haven't left a piece of gear hanging in the breeze halfway up the route!

SECONDING A CLIMB

11 ABSEILING

Abseiling is an important skill to master, as there are a number of reasons why it may be necessary to go down the rope. Probably the most usual will be in order to reach the bottom of the route, such as on a sea cliff where there is no path to the bottom, or on an outcrop where the descent path is a long way away. Another will be to retrieve gear. It can sometimes be tricky for your second to get the gear out when following the climb, and the gear may be best left in place and retrieved later by abseil, when you can use both hands and hang on the rope with no time pressure.

It is possible to climb at many venues without ever having to abseil, but the ability to abseil is part and parcel of becoming a rock climber.

It is important to distinguish between two different styles of abseiling.

Group abseil session
Here the main purpose is enjoyment, the abseil being the main objective of the day with lots of descents taking place. The session will be rigged so that the group has many turns at sliding down the rope, sometimes bouncing and sometimes past overhangs. The kit used will often be designed specifically for this type of use. The ropes may be of a rugged low-stretch variety, so avoiding them rubbing across edges and abrading, and helping to minimise erosion at the cliff edge. There will usually be someone with a safety rope as a back-up in case the abseiler lets go or loses control. The abseil device will normally be a chunky figure of eight or similar piece of kit. This is very controllable and has a large surface area, allowing maximum dissipation of the heat generated by friction when sliding down.

Personal abseil
This is the style used by the rock climber, and is the version we will concentrate on in this chapter. There will often be only one climbing rope available with no low-stretch rigging ropes in sight. The anchors that you use will have to be cunningly constructed, and may have to be fashioned in such a way that you can pull the rope down once you have descended. Bouncing, beloved of group abseilers, is very

hard on the anchors and is definitely not a good idea, and there will be no one standing by with a back-up safety rope. Finally, you will most likely use your belay device for the abseil, which is why it is important at the outset to choose one that will perform both jobs equally well.

A free abseil, where the climber's feet don't touch the rock – Hodge Close quarry, Lake District

Tip
....
If you do not have to retrieve the rope, it would be best to tie it off at the anchor to avoid any slippage. Simply tying a double bowline around the anchor (such as a tree), will work well, with the addition of a stopper knot, as this can be untied easily when finished with. Alternatively, if it is being clipped into a karabiner, a figure of eight tied at the centre point is fine.

ANCHORS

The anchor selected for the abseil must, beyond question, be solid. This applies to all anchors, but here there must be no doubt whatsoever that the anchor will not fall apart. All your weight will be on it and any failure will be catastrophic. Don't rush when selecting something suitable to use.

You will know, prior to descending, whether or not you will need to pull the rope through after you. This may be necessary on a sea cliff, for example, if you just have one rope and are going to use it for climbing as well. Alternatively, the rope may be staying in place, as when retrieving gear or when a second rope is available for the abseil.

Anchors can be constructed using either a single placement or more than one point.

Single anchor point

Single points will cover anchors such as trees, tree roots and boulders. It is quite easy to judge whether or not a tree is safe, but be wary of those growing on a barren flat cliff top as their roots may have little purchase. Roots can also be very strong, but may be rotten or have suffered the ignominy of many climbers over the years kicking them to test their strength – guaranteed to eventually compromise anchor potential. A high take-off point will always be desirable, and a tree may well offer this. However, make sure that there will be no significant increase in leverage on the trunk; if there is any doubt lower the attachment point. Retrieving the rope from around a tree is often quite a simple task, as the trunk offers little friction.

Spare a thought for the tree itself. If you feel that it is ideal to abseil from, many earlier climbers have probably thought so too, and there will be more to come. Many trees on crags have been killed by the action of the rope rubbing around the bark and cutting through it over time, so bear this in mind when setting up. Some padding, such as your empty gear rucksack placed at the back of the trunk, will help to prevent damage.

Boulders provide a couple of options for attachment in the form of spikes and threads. The rope can be looped over a spike, or passed through a thread, as when constructing belays (see Chapter 8). If you are going to leave the rope in place it will

A non-retrievable abseil rope tied high around a tree with a double bowline, making it easy to untie once loaded

(Right)
Spike anchor with a sling around it, holding the abseil rope through a karabiner

(Below right)
Multiple anchors brought down to one point for use as an abseil rope attachment point to access a climb. The equipment can be retrieved when you get back to the top of the route.

be a simple process to set up. However, if you need to retrieve the rope some thought needs to go into rigging the system. It is very unlikely, for instance, that you will be able to thread the rope between a couple of boulders and then be able to pull it down from below, as the friction would be too great. You would be very lucky to find a spike anchor that lets you do the same, as you need to take into account not just the rope running around the spike but also the points at which it touches along the top and over the edge of the cliff. In both these situations, furnishing the spike or thread with a long sling would be the answer, as your attachment would then be through a smooth karabiner with far less friction on the rope.

Multiple anchor points

Anchor systems using more than one point of attachment to the crag are quite common. Although a number of pieces of gear – for instance two wires and a rockcentric – may be used, they are best brought together to one point and the abseil rope attached to this. The method for bringing the anchors together is exactly the same as for equalising anchors (see Chapter 4), and the abseil rope will then be secured to them using a screwgate karabiner.

> ## Note
>
> Avoid using camming devices as anchors when setting up an abseil. As they can 'walk' into a crack under certain conditions – such as when the rope is tensed and released – they could move and possibly fail in some circumstances.

Tip

··········

Carrying the lead climbing rope, when abseiling on another one, can be awkward. Wrap up the rope by flaking, leaving longer ends than normal, around 2m. Put the rope behind your back with one tail over each shoulder, like a rucksack. Pass the tails under your arms, cross them over behind the rope and bring them round in front of you again. Tie them together with a suitable knot such as a reef knot or similar. The rope will stay on your back for the descent and won't flop around.

Note

··········

When at the cliff top watch out for any debris. Small rocks and stones litter many crags, and it is all too easy to knock something off with your foot or with coils of rope. If you should inadvertently do so, a loud shout of 'Below' will warn anyone who may be underneath.

Ensure your own security when deploying an abseil rope by clipping into an HMS with a clove hitch on the abseil rope/s

DEPLOYING THE ROPE

Once you have rigged the abseil anchor you need to get the rope down the crag, or 'deploy' it. It may be tempting to just pick it up and chuck it off, but this will almost certainly guarantee the nightmare of a knot appearing in it, enabling it to catch somewhere and become irretrievably jammed. A few moments sorting things out sensibly at the top of the cliff will make a huge difference to how easily the rope runs, and will be time well spent.

Firstly – and most important – look out for your own security as well as that of your partner. The edge of the crag may be slippery or overhung with grass or heather, so don't take any risks when sorting the rope out. It may be a good idea to tie yourself onto an appropriate part of the anchor when near the edge, done easily and quickly by tying a clove hitch into the abseil rope (into both sides of the rope if it is not tied off at the anchor), and clipping this into an HMS karabiner at your harness.

Before deploying the rope make sure that there is no one underneath, particularly climbing on any route down which you may be descending. Dropping a rope onto someone, or even very close to them, will lose you friends and is potentially quite dangerous. A visual check if possible, then a shout of 'Rope below' before deploying will warn people. If you are not sure the coast is clear don't throw the rope off; if it hits a climber the shock may cause him to fall off.

There are two ways of deploying the rope once you are happy that everything has been set up properly. If the route down is particularly steep, you may elect to let the rope run out through your hand and make its own way down the crag under its own weight. You will have to help it on its way initially, but gravity will very soon take over. This

Preparing the rope for throwing down the crag

11

ABSEILING

Tip

Having the centre of the rope marked is very useful, both for finding the middle when rigging an abseil and for coiling it up at the end of the day. Many manufacturers mark the middle using a special type of ink that won't harm the rope. If yours doesn't have this, or if it starts to fade over time, the same ink can be purchased from specialist climbing shops. Another possibility is to mark the centre with coloured sticky tape. Check with the rope manufacturer that the adhesive used is not going to react adversely with the rope fibres – specialised climbing tape is available for this purpose. Do not use commercially available fibre-tipped marker pens or similar.

method works well if there is no chance of the rope becoming snagged on the way down, but if conditions are not ideal a different method needs to be used. The most versatile is to flake the rope over your hand and then throw it down the crag, as follows:

1 Starting from the anchor end, flake the rope back and forward over your hand as if preparing to pack it away.
2 Once all the rope has been flaked, separate it so that you have half in each hand.
3 Throw the rope, from the hand holding the ends first, down the crag. In windy conditions it may be necessary to throw overarm forcefully. As these coils come off one hand, open the other so that the rope can peel off from there as well. This reduces the chance of the rope twisting and knotting.

Length of rope

Bear in mind the distance that you can abseil with your rope. If it is 50m long, you will be able to abseil a maximum of 25m, less a bit for connecting to the anchor. You need to be absolutely sure that the ends are touching the

Tip

Not only are low-stretch ropes less likely to abrade over an edge and are more resilient to repeated use, they are also often much cheaper than a good quality climbing rope. You may decide to invest in a length if you plan to do a number of abseils during the day, saving your dynamic rope from overuse and possible damage through repeated descents. This would be particularly useful if, for instance, you plan to spend a lot of time abseiling down sea cliffs.

(Top) **STEP 1**
Placing the abseil ropes into the device

(Bottom) **STEP 2**
The device clipped into the abseil loop, with the ropes correctly oriented

ground, or are on a substantial ledge if in a multi-pitch abseil situation. If there is any doubt, tie an overhand knot about 1m up from the end on each side of the rope. These knots will prevent you from abseiling off the end if you don't notice how far down you've travelled. They will also allow each side of the rope to untwist independently, stopping any kinks from building up, a possible problem if the ends are tied together.

USING A DEVICE FOR ABSEILING

It is most likely that you will use the device used for belaying as an abseil device. This gives you a lot of control and works in a fashion that doesn't cause the ropes to twist. We will assume that you are abseiling on two sections of the same rope (whether it is tied off at the anchor or not). The following procedure is the simplest preparation for descent:

1   Position yourself away from the cliff edge before connecting to the rope.
2   Clip an HMS screwgate karabiner to the abseil loop on your harness, but don't do it up yet.
3   Holding the belay/abseil device in the correct orientation for abseiling (check on the manufacturer's instructions), push a loop of rope through each of the two slots. Ensure that the rope is going through the top of the slot and out through the bottom (live rope above, dead rope below).
4   Keeping this orientation, clip the ropes and the device's retaining loop into the HMS karabiner and do it up.
5   Holding onto the dead rope with either one or both hands, weight the system to check that the orientation is correct. Note that this loading is *not* so that you can check the anchor – this should have been done thoroughly beforehand.
6   Make your way back towards the edge and over, paying the rope out as you go.

Keep your feet at twice hip width and start slowly at the top of an abseil

This process is quite simple and easy to undertake, and is how abseils are made the world over. However, it has one big drawback. If you let go of the dead rope during the descent there is nothing to stop you from crashing to the ground out of control. This is not a good prospect, so we need to devise a way of protecting the abseil with a 'dead-man's handle' system which will take over if we let go of the rope.

PROTECTING AN ABSEIL

There are a number of ways of doing this but we will look at using a prusik loop tied as a French prusik as the back-up, with the whole system being arranged so that it is clipped centrally into the harness.

1   The abseil device is connected to the abseil loop on the harness with an extension of 15–20cm. This can be achieved by using an extender of suitable length, or by looping a short sling around the abseil loop and clipping the ends together.
2   A French prusik is placed on the dead rope under the abseil device with four or five wraps around the rope and is also clipped to the abseil loop. Ensure that there is no way that this can reach and touch the device, which would render the system useless.
3   To descend, one hand holds the French prusik loosely and the other hand controls the dead rope and the rate

Tip

If you have ever taken part in a group abseil event you will have a good idea of how to position your body to maintain balance all the way down. Feet just over hip width apart, sitting back in your harness, upper body relaxed and legs straight will all help to make you feel more comfortable during the descent.

ABSEILING

11

at which it is fed through the abseil device. Make sure that you control your descent with the dead rope hand and not with the prusik, as this will become very jerky and difficult to control. The smoothest descent will be made with the rope falling between your legs, not off to one side.

4   If you wish to stop, release your grip on the French prusik which will then ride up slightly and grip the rope, stopping it from feeding through the device. You may wish to push it up slightly at first to help it tighten. You can now take your other hand off the dead rope.

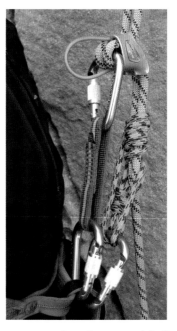

Set-up for a protected abseil

Note

If you need to stop for any time during your abseil, such as when retrieving gear, it is a good idea to back-up the French prusik. Taking two or three wraps of the dead rope around your thigh will do the job and ensure that should the prusik slip for some reason you will not slide any distance.

Note

It is important that screwgate karabiners are used for all connections to the abseil rig. If not available, two snapgate karabiners can be arranged so that they open in different directions.

Note

It is important that you use separate karabiners for the prusik and for the extender, if one is being used. If both are clipped into the same karabiner, there is a chance that the French prusik will touch the extender and not lock off, being pinched between the extender and the rope.

Tip

If you find that the descent is jerky you may be using a device with extra friction grooves, designed for use when belaying with thin ropes. Turning it around so that the grooves are away from the abseil rope and your controlling hand will help to smooth things out. If this does not work, adding a spare karabiner between the device and the karabiner to your harness might help, as this will prevent the two from jamming together, thus making the paying out of the rope easier.

Note

Abseiling is a technical procedure that needs to be practised. Do this where a mistake is not going to result in a bad accident – even rigging the rope around a tree in your back garden will allow you to go through the process of setting up the appropriate system before it is needed for real.

ITALIAN HITCH ABSEIL – WITHOUT A DEVICE

This should really be considered as an emergency procedure rather than a day-to-day method of abseiling. Imagine the scene: you are on the top of the crag and just about to make an abseil when you inadvertently drop your belay device and watch helplessly as it rolls away and drops over the edge. This leaves you with the rope and an empty HMS karabiner. Can you still abseil? You can – and this is where the Italian hitch comes in.

It works by the friction created by the rope rubbing around itself and over the curve at the end of a karabiner. Once in place, you can easily abseil with the hitch and it makes for a very controllable descent. The downside is that it tends to twist the rope a little. This isn't such a problem if the rope is going to be left in place, but can cause difficulty if it needs to be retrieved as any twists will have to be sorted out before pulling it down. Also it is very difficult to protect an abseil effectively when using an Italian hitch so you need to be absolutely sure that you have a good grip on the dead rope all the way down.

It is essential that the Italian hitch is connected to an HMS karabiner to allow the ropes to run unhindered. If a D-shape karabiner was used the ropes would not only squash into the tight bend at the top side of the back bar, stopping them from running smoothly, but may also prove to be irreversible if the hitch had to be inverted for some reason. You will probably have an HMS to hand, as it may well have been from here that your belay device so recently departed!

The arrangement of the Italian hitch abseil is as follows:

1   Clip the HMS onto the abseil loop of your harness. The widest end must be outermost and the back bar on the same side as your controlling hand, the one that will be holding the dead rope. If you are right handed clip the karabiner into the abseil loop with the gate opening to the left. If you are left handed, clip it so that the gate faces right.

11

ABSEILING

2 Tie an Italian hitch in the rope. If it is doubled, as will usually be the case, tie one large knot rather than two small separate ones, as they will cause the system to jam.

3 Clip the hitch into the karabiner and do up the screwgate. For a doubled rope, this will mean that four sections are clipped in together.

4 Hold onto the dead rope and lean back on the rope slightly to check that the whole rig will be loaded correctly whilst you abseil. It is essential that the dead rope is running across the back bar of the karabiner. If it were to run over the gate it could unscrew on the way down with disastrous consequences.

5 Descent is made by holding the dead rope and feeding it into the hitch at an appropriate rate.

Rope rigged for an abseil using the Italian hitch

With a standard Italian hitch – such as used for belaying – maximum friction is achieved by having both ropes parallel to each other (the dead rope next to the live rope). When abseiling this is often not possible, as the weight of the doubled ropes hanging down the crag makes lifting them up into a parallel position very awkward. However, the ropes will create plenty of friction on their own, so lifting them may not be necessary. Be very careful with thin and shiny ropes, as they will create little friction due to the fibres being 'slippery'. Also, the further you descend the less rope will be below you, and the faster you will go as you won't be helped by the weight of the rope – be warned!

Tip

The Italian hitch has a tendency to twist the rope when used for an abseil. If you then need to retrieve the rope making sure that you have untwisted it can be difficult. To solve this, clip a free-running karabiner onto the relevant side between the ropes above the Italian hitch as you abseil. This will be suspended above you by the ropes as you descend. Once down, untwist the ropes and the karabiner will slide down towards you. Once you have it you will know that all the twists have gone and the rope can be pulled down.

RETRIEVING THE ROPE

Once you are down – and assuming that you need the rope to be pulled down after you – the next job is to retrieve it. If you have planned ahead and thought about issues such as friction points, which side of the rope to pull and have made sure there are no twists, there should not be much of a problem. However, it pays to make sure that it will all run smoothly. Once the first person has reached the ground, get him to give the rope a test pull to make sure that it is running fine. You can watch from above to make sure that all is OK, and will be able to make any fine adjustments from there.

If once you are down the rope seems to be stuck, this is probably due to the friction caused by it running across the rock. Grasp one of the ends and maintain a steady downward pressure on it. Now have your partner 'flick' the rope upwards in a series of sine-wave type loops. This will lift it away from the rock and hopefully allow it to be retrieved. When your partner comes to the end of the rope he throws it up as high as possible into the air whilst you continue pulling, which should let it run through the anchor and fall to the ground.

Tip

Take great care when pulling ropes through. There may be debris lying on a ledge or the top, and the rope could dislodge some. Wearing a helmet is a very sensible precaution. Ensure that the rope will not hit anyone climbing or walking nearby. If there is anyone in the near vicinity it would be courteous to wait for them to move away and at least warn them of what you are about to do. A shout of 'Rope below' will alert others in the area of the forthcoming hazard.

11.

ABSEILING

Abseiling above the sea requires a cool head

MULTI-PITCH CLIMBS

You may find yourself faced with the prospect of abseiling from a multi-pitch climb, where the rope will not reach the ground in one go but ends up on a suitable ledge. You may know about this in advance from the guidebook, or it may happen unexpectedly, perhaps if the route you are on is proving too hard, you are off line, experiencing bad weather or imminent darkness.

Planned descent

In this case you should be prepared for the descent. Popular routes that have more than one abseil to reach the bottom will often make use of suitable ledges with handy spikes or trees as abseil anchors, and these will sometimes have chains around them through which you can thread the rope. It is essential that you check every part of the anchor before using it, and if in any doubt either back it up with some of your own gear, or choose another abseil point.

Unplanned descent

You will have to think carefully through the options and plan meticulously what needs to be done. Although the climb may have taken you past suitable ledges, these may not have good anchor points from which you can retrieve the rope. In that case, you will need to provide your own anchors and will have to abandon any gear used. In the best-case scenario this may be just a sling and karabiner, threaded between a couple of boulders and arranged so that the rope can be pulled through without any problem. However, you may also need to link up two or three anchors and bring them down to one, meaning that you lose a number of wires as well as karabiners and a sling. It is extremely important that you err on the side of safety. If an extra wire and karabiner will hugely increase the security of the system, then put them in place. The small amount of money that you are going to lose pales into insignificance compared to the potential loss of life that could result from skimping on kit.

Setting up the abseil device

It is a very good idea to protect an abseil in a multi-pitch situation. The system outlined above gives an excellent method of security, but for a multi-pitch descent we may want to tweak it a little. The system described is basically the same, but uses a sling for connection to the abseil device, as well as providing a cow's-tail extension for security. This can be clipped in to subsequent anchor points during the descent to protect you when pulling the rope through.

Note

When retrieving the rope in a multi-pitch situation be very careful not to drop it after pulling it through. If there is any chance of this tie one end onto an appropriate part of the anchor before starting to pull it down; if you do let go at least it won't be lost.

1 Using a 120cm sling, a lark's-foot is used to connect it to your abseil loop.
2 Tie an overhand knot around 20–30cm from your harness. Make sure that the sewn section of the sling is not part of this knot.
3 The short loop coming from your harness is used to hold the abseil device.
4 Using a prusik loop, tie a French prusik and put it on the dead rope, then connect it to your harness with a screwgate in the usual manner.
5 The longer loop, reaching to the far end of the sling, can be furnished with a screwgate karabiner. This is the cow's-tail and will be useful for clipping into anchors.

When you arrive at the next ledge, the screwgate can be clipped into an appropriate point on the anchor before you unclip from the abseil rope, and so you are connected to a part of the system at all times. When descending, the cow's-tail screwgate can be placed in a number of places.

- If long enough, it can clip onto a gear loop, keeping it out of the way.
- Another option will be to clip it onto the abseil loop below all the other screwgates.
- The best place may be to clip it above the device onto one of the abseil ropes, so that it is free running and towed down by you as you descend. This is very helpful as it can sometimes be awkward remembering which side of the rope to pull during retrieval. Clipping the karabiner to the correct rope before abseiling down this will serve as a reminder.

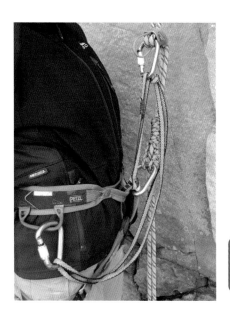

(Above) **Abseil set-up using a sling as a cow's-tail**

(Below) **Abseil rig and cow's-tail set-up, with the karabiner clipped into the abseil rope and running freely**

JOINING ROPES

If you are climbing with a single rope this should not be a consideration. However, there is a chance that your rope may become damaged in a rock fall and you have to tie the two sections together to abseil. There is also a chance that you will be climbing with double ropes, or with three people, thus having a rope from leader to second and another from second to third. If you are able to use two ropes together you will be able to abseil twice as far as you could with just one rope doubled up.

Joining the ropes is something that you need to get right! The two most popular options are given here in order of preference.

Double fisherman's knot

The first is to join them with a double fisherman's knot. However, when loaded this knot can become very difficult to untie. To help tie a reef knot in the ropes first, which will stop the fisherman's from sliding together and jamming. Overall this is a very secure method of joining the ropes, and usually the first choice.

(Right)
Reef knot tied between a double fisherman's

(Below)
Joining the ropes using two overhand knots butted together

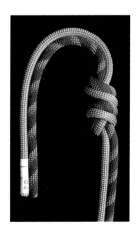

One slight drawback of this method is that the knot is very bulky. On technical terrain there is a chance that it might catch during retrieval, causing the rope to become stuck. If this is likely an overhand knot could be the better option.

Overhand knot

This type of overhand knot should be tied twice for security. It will present a smooth profile to the rock when being pulled down, with less chance of getting stuck. Start by tying an overhand knot in both ropes together. Take a moment to seat the knot neatly, pulling on the ends to get it tight. Tie a second overhand knot so that it butts up against the first, neaten this and pull it tight. It is important that the tails left after the knot is complete are no less than 50cm long.

A version of this with one overhand knot has been used for years by climbers and Alpinists. Although minimalist, it has the least chance of becoming stuck during retrieval.

However, the double version mentioned will do nicely for all the applications we are likely to come across on most outcrops and cliffs.

A SEA-CLIFF ABSEIL

I make no apologies for including another anecdote based at Swanage. As this is where I started climbing, equipped with as little knowledge as it is possible to have and still survive, it is also where some of my biggest epics occurred.

A high proportion of the routes entail an abseil descent to start with, in order to access a ledge or boulders at the bottom. This is all well and good providing you can climb back out again. Some areas, such as the Boulder Ruckle section, require you to be competent at leading VS or higher in order to safely make it back to the top of the cliff.

On one of our first forays into the Ruckle the long-suffering Simon and I abseiled in, pulled the rope down after us and consulted the guidebook. We discovered that we had arrived at the wrong point, with the climb we wanted out of reach around a tide-swept corner. Above us were routes we had no chance of leading; they looked ferocious and the guidebook description would have given the stoutest person nightmares. Having no way out, and little idea of the state of the tide, we were completely marooned. To cut a long story short, by pure chance a couple of local 'hard men' arrived and let us use their abseil rope as a means of ascent. We had practised prusiking many times (having seen Clint Eastwood use it in *The Eiger Sanction*) and were convinced that it would be of benefit at some time. And so it was. Simon made his way up, so very slowly, and then belayed me to the top.

The lessons kept being learned. If abseiling into a sector that has no easy way out, leave the abseil rope in place. Consider tying it off at the top to make prusiking easier if you need to get out, and perhaps pad the section of rope that runs over the edge to protect it. Carry the means of climbing up the rope, such as prusik loops, Tiblocs or similar, and know how to use them. Finally, make absolutely sure via the guidebook that you are descending into the right place, as to correct this error later may be extremely difficult, or even impossible, to do – not to say embarrassing.

Note

It may seem that a figure of eight, instead of an overhand knot, would be a better alternative. However, it has been shown that this knot fails at a far lesser load than the overhand knot, as it can roll out along the rope and completely untie. **Do not tie one when joining ropes together!**

11

ABSEILING

Note
. . . .

The klemheist is a useful knot as it grips the climbing rope tightly when you pull on it. However, unlike the French prusik, it cannot be released downwards whilst under load. This makes it suitable as the attachment to your harness when ascending the rope, as you do not want the knot to slip unexpectedly, something that could happen if a French prusik were used. However, the latter is fine to use for your foot attachment, as it is easier to move and any slippage will not be a major problem.

PRUSIKING

It is useful to practise this style of ascending the rope in advance, particularly if you are going to be abseiling into sea cliffs, where the only way out is to climb up again. It can be carried out with two prusik loops or with a couple of purpose-designed rope clamps, such as Tiblocs.

If using prusik loops attach a klemheist to your abseil loop with a screwgate karabiner. Place the second loop, tied as a French prusik, below it. Clip a 120cm sling onto this. Placing a foot in the sling, push down to take the stretch out of the rope. Slide the klemheist up until it is snug, and then sit back in the harness. You can now slide the French prusik on the sling up. Stand up in the sling once more, slide the klemheist up, sit back in the harness so that you can slide the French prusik up, and keep repeating this process.

After a couple of metres, tie a clove hitch in the rope below your prusiks and clip it into an HMS karabiner onto your abseil loop. This will serve as a back-up should a prusik slip, and the spare rope can be taken through it at various stages as you make your way up.

Mechanical devices are very useful if you think that ascending the rope may be a possibility. They grip the rope tightly but slide up smoothly when needed.

Klemheist knot *(left)* **and Tibloc jamming device** *(right)*

Take time to practise prusiking well before it is needed. A handy tree will be a good place to start, or a low section of cliff. If using a tree, make sure that you have worked out how to get down again!

There are a number of common problems that are associated with abseiling, and the main ones are listed below.

PROBLEM	REMEDY
Anchor failure.	Double-checking of anchor, backing it up if necessary, and choosing an alternative if there is any doubt.
Abseiling off the end of the rope.	Check the rope reaches the ground before abseiling. Tie knots in the end to avoid abseiling off.
Jamming of abseil device.	Commonly caused by loose hair or clothing. Check that nothing is flapping around and able to catch in the device.
Back-up French prusik too tight or ineffective.	Practise in a safe location and find out how many wraps it will take for your prusik to grip properly before having to use it for real.
Abseil rope irretrievable.	Extend the anchor so that the rope is nearer the departure point. Test-pull it while still at the top to check that it runs OK.

12 MULTI-PITCH ROUTES

(Opposite) **The first pitch of 'Black mamba', VS 4c, a 1000ft route at Creag an Dubh-loch**

Fairly early on in your climbing career you will probably find yourself setting out to tackle a multi-pitch route (a slightly misleading term in that such a climb may have as few as two or as many as 10 – or more – pitches!).

Some short outcrops can contain routes with more than one pitch. Although the height of the cliff may be less than a rope length, the route may zigzag or dodge under an overhang, thus making a two-pitch route more sensible in order to avoid rope drag and communication problems.

Most multi-pitch routes, however, will have more than two pitches. These need not be of any difficulty, and there are a great number of low-graded routes on crags and mountains that will provide easy but absorbing days out for anyone just starting out on their climbing career. These routes will either be continuous, with stances taken on appropriate ledges at certain points along the way, or may include a bit of walking. Mountain routes in particular – and especially those in the easier grades – may involve arriving at a large grassy ledge, bringing up your second and then having to move to a different part to climb the next pitch.

CHOOSING A ROUTE

Picking a route suitable for your first multi-pitch lead can seem a little daunting, but should not be a problem if you consider the following:

- Crag or mountain
- Weather
- Gear
- Distance to walk in
- Length of route and climbing time
- Descent
- Distance to walk off
- Available daylight hours.

Crag or mountain

I would recommend a low-level crag for your first trip or two. It is much better to learn how to deal with multi-pitch climbing in a reasonably controlled situation rather than on a windswept mountain route.

Weather

This will be a relevant factor for any day on the crag, but on longer routes finding out what the weather has in store becomes crucial. Choosing a mountain ridge route on a wet and windy day would not be sensible; neither will a south-facing crag in the middle of a heat wave in summer. The type of rock may also have a bearing: choosing a slippery surface such as mica schist to climb on in the wet would not be the best decision, whereas a grippy rock such as granite will offer a lot more security if the weather is looking a little dodgy.

Gear

By the time you head out for your first multi-pitch route you will have a very good idea as to what technical kit is going to be useful. I would suggest taking an extra couple of long slings with screwgates attached, as these are always very useful. Helmets are essential, particularly in a mountain situation, as the chance of debris being dislodged is quite high. Think about how you are going to carry the kit. Each of you will probably start off with a rucksack for the walk in. Once geared up, it may be worth whoever is seconding carrying one of these with all the spare kit, including the second rucksack rolled up, so that nothing is left behind.

Walk in/walk off/length of route/timing/daylight hours

These factors all have a bearing on each other. If daylight hours are short, such as in late autumn, planning to climb a route that will take two hours to walk in, five hours to climb, an hour to descend and two hours to walk out would not be a sensible objective. You may decide to walk in early, or accept that you will be walking out late, with a head torch each, but as the chance of becoming benighted on the route is quite high the sensible option would be to choose something else.

Descent

It is astonishing that climbers don't give more thought to this prior to setting out. There will have been, worldwide, far more epics in descent than on the actual climb. So how do you get down? Do you need to abseil or is walking off the norm? Your guidebook should give you the necessary information, and you will probably find that walking off is, in the majority of cases, the most usual finish to the day. So do you need to change your rock shoes for walking boots? Does it require navigation or complex route finding? This all needs to be sorted out prior to reaching the top of the route and saying 'Oops – what do we do now?'

CLIMBING THE ROUTE

There are two different methods of climbing multi-pitch routes: 'leading on' and 'leading through'. On a single-pitch climb one person leads the route from bottom to top, as it would obviously be impractical for any changes in lead to take place. On a multi-pitch route, however, things can be a bit more fluid.

- **Leading on** means that the same person leads consecutive pitches. The leader climbs the first pitch, belays, brings up the second and then leads the next pitch.
- **Leading through** ('swinging leads') means that one climber leads the first pitch, belays the second who, on arrival at the stance, takes over the gear and leads the next pitch.

There are a number of variations, and whether you alternate pitches or lead the whole route can be decided as you go. For instance, you may lead through for the first couple of pitches but, if you are the more confident climber and the next couple of pitches are hard, you may decide to lead on. Once you have got past the hard section, you could go back to leading through again.

Depending on the technique used, the ropework styles at the individual stances will differ slightly, mainly in the way that the belayer rigs the system. It is very easy to just anchor yourself and haul your mate up, swap gear and watch him launch himself up the next pitch, but doing this without thinking through the relevant rope systems could cause tangles and all sorts of problems, and the main points are covered below. Remember to practise on a short section of crag before committing yourself to a long route and finding that the system you've chosen doesn't work too well.

Anchor considerations

In an ideal world perfect anchor options present themselves at every stance. Unfortunately it is rarely so, and we need to think through the optimum system in each situation. Ideally – and certainly for leading on – a single anchor point is desirable. This may be achieved by simply having a sling around a suitable boulder, or by equalising anchors with a sling (see Chapter 4). You should be familiar with the relevant methods before having to rig the systems for real.

Leading on

The same climber will be leading consecutive pitches. A single attachment point is a real boon here as it makes

By following this routine you ensure that you are both connected to the system at all times, either by being on belay or clipped into the anchor. Don't ever be tempted to wander about on a ledge unclipped, unless it is quite large and you are well away from the edge. Even so, it may be worth having a rope loosely attached to the anchor.

Belaying from a stance with a pre-placed runner for the next pitch

changing things around at the stance so much easier. A classic stance management would be as follows:

1 The leader climbs the route and belays, using either a single anchor or multiple points brought down to one.
2 He brings up the second.
3 The second positions himself on the stance in an appropriate place for belaying the next pitch, with his braking arm away from the direction of load (away from the cliff). Taking the rope from just below the leader's belay device he ties a clove hitch and clips it into the same anchor.
4 The leader can now take off his belay device, as both climbers are safe.
5 The leader retrieves any necessary gear from the second, stripped out from the previous pitch.
6 The rope will need to be 'turned round'. At the moment the rope to the second is coming out of the top of the pile so the second runs it though, starting at his attachment point, piling it on the ledge in a suitable position, just off to his braking arm side.
7 This rope will come tight on to the anchor, and from there onto the leader. The second now puts the leader on belay.
8 The leader, having checked that everything is ready, can now unclip from the anchor and start up the next pitch.

Leading through
This is perhaps the most usual way for a pair of climbers to share the leading on a route (often the best bit!). The stance set-up will be slightly different to that used when leading on.

1 The leader reaches the stance and belays himself as above.
2 He pre-places the first piece of protection for the next pitch, and clips the rope in. The rope runs from his belay device up and through the gear and then down to the second. The second climbs up to the stance, with the belayer facing inwards, as any load, in the event of a fall, will be coming from the pre-placed gear.
3 As the second will now become the leader, he may elect to not clip into the anchor. Although there is no problem in doing so, a quicker method will be to tie him off at the belay device. Taking a large bight of rope from just by the device on the dead-rope side, tie a large overhand knot in it with at least a 30cm tail. This will provide ample back-up should the leader slip, as the knot will immediately jam in the belay device.

4 The new leader now collects all the relevant gear from the new second.

5 Having checked that everything is ready, the belayer unties the overhand knot and the leader starts up the next pitch.

Pre-placing the first piece of gear for the next pitch makes a huge difference to the smooth running of the stance, as the position of the belayer and the orientation of the belay device will not have to be altered. If it is not possible to do this, another couple of tasks have to be performed:

1 Once the second arrives at the stance, he clips into the anchor with a separate screwgate.

2 The belayer takes the second off his device and repositions himself as appropriate. This may just be turning his body around from an 'arm inward' to an 'arm outward' position.

An overhand knot, tied below the belay device, serves as an effective back-up

3 The rope is reconnected to the belay device in the correct manner. When the leader was belaying the second the dead rope will have come out from the top of the device. It now needs to come out of the bottom, as he is now belaying a new leader above him.

4 Once he is back on belay, the new leader can take his rope off the anchor and start to climb.

Note

It is very useful to pre-place the first runner of the next pitch. It not only makes the rope management much easier at the stance, but also immediately provides a way of preventing a fall factor of 2, which would otherwise produce a high loading on the anchor system.

Note

Remember to swap gear at the stance if you are changing over, and to collect any stripped out of the last pitch if you are leading on. Once tied in there is no reason for the belayer to have any spare kit on him, such as slings, so make sure that you have as much as you need for the next pitch.

MULTI-PITCH ROUTES

Steep, multi-pitch crack climbing in America. 'Supercrack of the Desert', Moab, Utah, 5.10.

THE MULTI-PITCH TALE

One of the great joys of multi-pitch climbing is the time that you spend with a good companion. Sometimes, however, that time is a little too long, and a slight epic results. Such an event happened on one of my first ever multi-pitch routes, climbed in North Wales. It was early in the season and we had totally misjudged the amount of daylight available. Climbing, chatting and, I am very sure, poor technique, meant that night was upon us quicker than we had anticipated, leaving us with one final pitch to complete in almost total darkness.

Head torches were still a dream: surely 'real' climbers didn't carry them (and our student grant wouldn't stretch to the expense anyway). We had ignored not only the time of sunset but also the consequent effect that this would have upon our intended evening out with friends.

It was almost impossible to see the way ahead on the last short pitch. Although very easy by comparison to the rest of the route, the lack of light made progress very difficult. Luckily Simon had a lighter to hand. Using this I was able to see my way up the section, flicking the lighter so that the spark lit up the rock for a nanosecond, just enough for me to get my bearings. Attempts at climbing up with the flame alight were useless, as the slight breeze immediately put paid to that idea. I made my way up the last few feet of the climb by creating a flash of light, remembering where the holds were, groping in the dark for them, moving up, flashing again and so on. The idea of placing protection was abandoned, as arranging any sort of gear in those conditions would have been impossible.

Once I had reached the top it was Simon's turn to come up. He didn't have the luxury of a lighter, but did have the use of a tight rope coming from above, allowing him to climb in reasonable safety, if not style. I was pleased that he didn't fall off, as I had been unable to find any sort of usable anchor and had simply wrapped my legs around a boulder to prevent me being pulled off the cliff.

The way down was lit by a willowy moon, luxury considering that the last pitch of the route – some 30 easy feet in height – had taken over an hour to accomplish. A further three hours of stumbling and we ▶

◀ were down at the road, with an hour of fruitless hitching seeing us back at the campsite well after our friends had returned from the pub. We were just too tired to care.

The moral? Check out the route, the grade and the length, as well as access to and from it. Relate that to the competence levels of you and your partner and your estimated climbing speed. Leave in plenty of time, know when darkness is due and carry a head torch, even if your climb is planned to finish some time before dusk. Putting these elements together will help you to avoid the chance of becoming benighted on a route. It will also help you to avoid that most appalling of consequences – a week of mockery from your so-called mates.

EXTRA GEAR

The technical gear required does not differ from that used on single-pitch climbs. However, you will have to take a few extra items with you on routes that take a lot of time or are in a mountainous region, as follows:

- **Waterproofs** Mountain weather is very change-able, so be prepared.
- **Spare fleece** for the same reason as above.
- **Hat and gloves** The temperature may be a lot lower higher up, or the wind may increase, so make sure you keep warm and comfortable; being cold and miserable will not enhance your day.
- **Head torch** Essential to ensure a safe descent if the day is short or the route is long.
- **Map and compass** You may need to navigate down, and even if you start climbing in clear weather the cloud may roll in later in the day.
- **Food and drink** A snack or two stashed in a pocket will be welcome after an hour or two of climbing. If the route is to take any substantial amount of time, pack a reasonable amount of food and set aside time to eat it. Carrying water or other liquid to drink is important, especially on hot days.
- **Sun hat and sun cream** These can be essential. Spending a couple of hours on a south-facing crag in the full glare of the sun can cause all sorts of problems, so be prepared.

Tip

If you have a definite route in mind – which will take most of the day – photocopy the relevant page from the guide-book and take that with you instead of carrying the book itself. Make two copies and give one to your partner, folded into a plastic bag and stashed in a pocket. If you lose the first one, or it gets sodden in a downpour, you have a back-up.

12

MULTI-PITCH ROUTES

13 TOP- AND BOTTOM-ROPING

(Opposite) **Slab-climbing on a top rope on 'Fallen slab', V.Diff., Portland**

These are methods by which the rope is set up so that leading does not have to take place. They are often used at the end of a day's climbing, when the team might wish to attempt something harder than their normal leading grade, or perhaps as a warm-up activity early on. The difference is as follows:

- **Top-roping** The belayer controls the system from the top of the crag.
- **Bottom-roping** The belayer runs everything from the bottom of the crag.

Top-roping will usually require the use of a single rope whereas bottom-roping will often necessitate two, one to set up the rigging side and the second as the climbing rope. Finance and practicalities – such as whether you have one or two ropes to hand – will often be the deciding factors as to which one to go for. They both have an equal place in rock climbing and this chapter will cover both methods.

TOP-ROPING
This is essentially the same set-up as for a leader who has led a route, tied on at the top and is bringing up his second. The difference is that the route has not been led, with the belayer getting to the top of the crag (hopefully via some sensible means such as a footpath!), anchoring himself in place and throwing the rope down to the climber who then ties on.

One of the advantages of a top rope is that a direct belay set-up can be used easily (see Chapter 8). This has the advantage of allowing the belayer to be remote from the belay system but still protected by it, letting him control the rope as his partner ascends, but not be pulled about by it if he falls. This is a good idea if the route being climbed is quite hard and a number of falls, or at least 'dangles', are likely to be taken.

BOTTOM-ROPING
This is a little trickier and more time-consuming to set up, but is a good method if you have a second rope available

Note

As it is very unlikely that you will be belayed whilst setting up either a top- or bottom-rope rig, it is really important that you are aware of your own security when moving around near the edge of the crag. Tie onto an anchor if in any doubt.

for rigging. If not, it is still possible to run a bottom rope on a climb as long as the route is not too long. One of the advantages of a bottom rope is that the belayer can see the entire climb, which may be difficult with a top-rope set-up. It also means that the belayer is right next to the climber as he starts. If he is less experienced the belayer is there not only to tie him onto the rope but also to call out advice as he makes his way up.

Once the climber has reached the karabiners at the top of the route, there are two options.

The climber is lowered back to the ground This will usually be the best plan when climbing with a novice. If he is lowered back down he will not end up in a lead situation above the karabiners, making his way over the top edge of the crag. Falling from here would be scary (although should be safe as he will be on belay). Getting him to touch the

Tricky moves can be practised in relative safety on a top or bottom rope

karabiners at the top and then be lowered to the ground ensures that he is secure from above all the way up and down, and will make the whole climb more relaxing for him.

The climber continues up You may elect to climb up and past the karabiners holding the bottom rope in place, and onto the top of the crag. Only do this if the whole rig is sited right on the very edge of the cliff so that you are in a lead situation for just a short distance before gaining the flat ground. Doing this is quite common if a number of routes are going to be bottom-roped. The last person up, usually the more competent, can climb up and over, and then move the set-up to the next route. He can then walk down or, if the rig and top of the crag are ideal, climb down over the edge and be lowered. Extreme care must be taken when doing this, as a slip when re-rigging or a mistake by the belayer could be disastrous. Double-check everything; if there is any doubt simply walk down.

Rigging
We will look at the two most common methods of rigging a bottom rope. One uses just the climbing rope, and the second utilises a second rope to make rigging easier and a little more versatile.

Single-rope method This is only really of use for a short period of time and when few falls are likely to be taken. Falling on the rope – which is your climbing rope and also part of the rigging system over the cliff edge – won't do it much good. It will suffer bouncing under bodyweight and possibly become damaged if the edge is sharp and not well padded. However, for a short period of time, perhaps a climb or two to round off your day, and where the cliff is of no great height, it is quite appropriate.

We will assume here that two anchor points are being used at the top of the crag. A similar system can be set up if just one is used, such as a large tree. Bear in mind that the more anchor points the less the length of the route that can be climbed, as the rope will be used for rigging as well as climbing.

1   Select your two anchor points and equip them with appropriate gear, along with two screwgate karabiners.
2   Tie a figure of eight on the bight on one end of the rope, and clip this into an anchor.
3   At the edge of the cliff, looking out for your own security, place a loop of rope, taken from the first anchor, over the edge. Estimate how much rope will be taken up with a knot, and tie a figure of eight in it. Check the

TOP- AND BOTTOM-ROPING

length again, with the knot hanging over the edge in an appropriate position.

4   Take the rope from the other side of the knot and go back to the second anchor. Clip it in with either a clove hitch or figure of eight. The rope should now be running from each of the anchors across to the knot over the edge in a 'V'.

5   A short distance up from the knot over the edge, perhaps 1m, tie another figure of eight to link the ropes. This will serve to direct the two sides of the rigging system over the lip together, making protecting and padding it much easier. It can be adjusted into its final position once the rest of the rigging is complete.

6   Clip two screwgate karabiners into the loop made by the figure of eight. Arrange them so that they open in opposite directions, and so that the locking sleeve closes towards the bottom. If the sleeve closes towards the top, there is a chance of it vibrating open during use.

7   You now need to organise the climbing section of the rope. Feed the end over the cliff until it is on the ground. Clip the rope into the two screwgates, grip the rope tight so that it doesn't slide, and feed it down on the other side of the karabiners. It will now run up from the ground, through the two karabiners and back down to the ground. From here, it will run up again to the top of the crag and to the second anchor point. This section of rope, once it is all set up, can be ignored.

8   It is important that the ropes from the anchors share the load equally when the climbing rope is hanging in the right position. Adjust them now, as the weight of the rope will make it easier to get this right.

9   It is worth placing some padding, such as an empty rucksack, under the rope at the edge of the cliff to prevent rubbing. Clip a spare karabiner onto the rucksack shoulder straps or haul loop and then to the rigging side of the rope, so that it can't get knocked over the edge accidentally.

10 Make a final check that all the screwgates are done up, the anchors are sound and that it is all running in the correct direction, and the system is complete.

Using a second rope If you are going to do a lot of bottom-roping, perhaps with a number of friends, or the climbs in your area are too long for a single rope, a second rope is a very good idea. This could be dynamic, stretchy like your lead rope, but a better choice would be to buy a low-stretch rope, designed for rigging climbs. This type is less

Tip

When dealing with any type of bottom-rope rig make sure that you can see the karabiners through which the rope is running from where you are going to belay. If you can there is little chance of twists or snags jamming the system up.

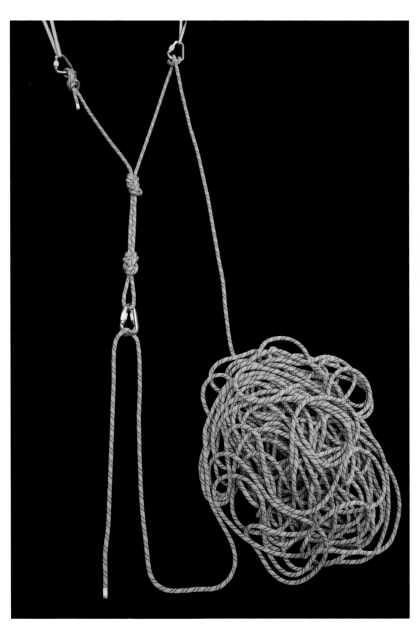

elastic than a climbing rope, so will wear less at the cliff edge. It will also cause less erosion at the cliff top, a real problem with soft rock such as sandstone, where loaded ropes can literally saw a few centimetres into the rock. Another, quite major consideration, is that they are usually much cheaper than a decent lead rope.

Completed rig for a bottom rope constructed from just the main lead rope

Bottom-rope rig using two ropes

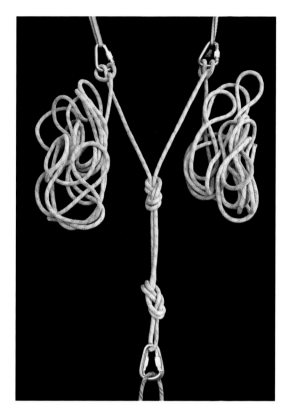

We will again assume that there are two anchor points, each equipped appropriately and with a screwgate karabiner clipped in.

1. At the middle of the low-stretch rope (the 'rigging rope') tie a figure of eight on the bight.
2. A short distance along from that, perhaps 1m, tie another figure of eight as mentioned for the single-rope system.
3. Clip two screwgates into this, arranged as before, facing in opposite directions with the sleeves screwing downwards to lock.
4. Uncoil your climbing rope and find the middle. Clip this into the two screwgates and do them up.
5. Lower the climbing rope down to the ground. Take care when doing this, and check with others in your group that it is clear before you do so. Make sure that you hold onto the rigging rope, which is not clipped into anything at this point. Not having it tied off makes things a lot quicker and easier to set up. If there is any question about you being able to hold it, clip it in.

Tip

With any bottom-roping rig there will always be some stretch in the system. Have someone pull hard on the ropes at the bottom to help 'bed them in'; if any fine adjustment is needed carry it out while still at the top.

6   The weight of the climbing rope makes the next bit easy. Adjust the knot and karabiners holding the climbing rope until they are in an appropriate position over the edge. Now, keeping them in place, walk back to the first anchor and clip the rope in with a clove hitch and adjust it so that the rope is snug.

7   Now take the other rope from the higher figure of eight and go to the second anchor, clip it in with a clove hitch and adjust it.

8   Place some padding (such as a rucksack) at the point where the rope runs over the cliff edge.

9   Tidy up the top of the crag by piling the unused rigging rope at the side of each anchor. Make a final check that all the screwgates are done up, that the anchors are sound and that it is all running in the correct direction, and the system is complete.

This makes for a very good system that is easily and quickly rigged. The advantage of having two clove hitches is that the system can be extensively fine-tuned and adjusted so that the karabiners supporting the climbing rope are in the optimum position. It is also relatively easy to move the rig to an adjoining route, simply requiring the adjustment of the clove hitches rather than any extensive re-rigging.

Note

When using a low-stretch rope for rigging, if the clove hitches are near the ends of it tie a couple of overhand knots around the load rope to lock them off and stop any chance of them slipping. Alternatively, extend the anchor with a sling.

Note

Consider the needs and wishes of other crag users. There may be other people around who want to climb the route you have set up, so check that they don't mind you carrying on. Remember that crag etiquette dictates that a couple leading a route will always take precedence over a group top- or bottom-rope set-up, so be prepared to move your ropes out of the way if someone wants to climb. You can pull them up to the top and wait for the climbing team to finish, then drop them back down again.

TOP- AND BOTTOM-ROPING

Tip

If you plan to do a lot of bottom-roping it would be worth getting some type of rope protector. These can be bought commercially, or you can make your own very cheaply. A piece of carpet, say 50–60cm square, is ideal, perhaps an off-cut from a carpet showroom. Make a small hole in one side and thread in a piece of strong string or an old sling. A karabiner can be clipped to this, and then used to secure it in position. An addition would be to use a prusik loop as well, which could be wound around the rigging rope at the desired point, with the karabiner and carpet being clipped into this.

Appendix 1
FALL FACTORS AND FORCES

FALL FACTORS

It is important to have an understanding of how fall factors are calculated in order to understand how critical the positioning of key runners is in relation to the load exerted on the system in the event of a fall.

Under normal climbing circumstances, the fall factor can range from 0 to 2, with the lower the factor the better the outcome. It is calculated by the following equation:

Fall factor = length of fall ÷ length of rope paid out

Let's look at a multi-pitch scenario. If the leader has left a stance and led out 5m of rope with no runners in place and falls off, he will fall 10m. Using the above equation gives us $10 \div 5 = 2$, thus a fall factor of 2. This creates an extremely high loading on the anchor and belay system, and is to be avoided at all costs. Placing a piece of gear as soon as he leaves the stance would help reduce the fall factor, thus reducing the loading on the anchor and belay system and greatly increasing his safety.

If the leader has climbed up 5m, placing a runner 2.5m above the stance, and subsequently falls off – a 5m fall in total – the fall factor is calculated in the same manner: $5 \div 5 = 1$. This gives a fall factor of 1, much better for both anchors and climber.

Although a fall factor higher than 1 is only possible in a multi-pitch situation (because on a single-pitch route the ground breaks the fall), it's important to think about short routes as well. A fall factor of 1 is still huge, as the leader will have dropped from his highest point to where he started climbing from, so the frequent placement of good runners is key to reducing the factor and ensuring safety.

KILONEWTONS AND FORCES

It is useful to have a basic understanding of forces and how they affect climbers. The Newton is the unit of force, and where the loading on a system will be quite high – such as in a fall situation – kiloNewtons (kN) are used. One kiloNewton is the force exerted by a 100kg climber (a big person, but used here for ease of calculation!) hanging on a

It's always best to heed local warnings!

climbing system and being affected by the pull of gravity. Any extra loading – such as when a leader is being lowered to the ground from part way up a route and thus bouncing on the rope slightly – will immediately increase this force (in this case on the top runner).

Climbing gear is tested and rated according to its strength in kiloNewtons. A typical karabiner, for instance, may be rated to hold a minimum of 25kN. This will err on the conservative side with safety in mind, and its actual strength could be far greater. Under normal usage it will be impossible for a climber to put a load of 25kN onto a piece of gear.

The energy created by a fall will be absorbed by the elasticity of the rope and the belay system, otherwise the leader could be injured. The ability of the rope to absorb energy by stretching slightly is key to this process. 'Dynamic' belaying – where a little rope is allowed to slip through the belay device before it is locked off – will also help to reduce the resulting load on the climber, known as the 'impact force'. The lower the impact force the better for all concerned. Ropes are tested to a maximum of 12kN, as this is seen to be the highest impact force that the human body can take. When new a good technical rope will have an impact force of around 7 or 8kN.

The 'peak impact force' is where the above calculations come together: the load on the belay, runner and rope system at the moment of highest loading. With a fall factor of 1 or less (the norm for sensible climbing with prudent gear placements) the peak impact force on the top runner will be somewhere between 3 and 7kN. This top runner will have to take the force generated by the falling leader and by the belayer holding the rope. Due to the friction through the karabiner on the top runner – the 'pulley effect' – the load on it will be around 1.6 times that exerted on the fallen leader. It is due to this pulley effect that the load on the belayer will be lower than the impact force on the climber.

As ropes age and are fallen on, they lose some of their elasticity and become less able to absorb energy produced during a fall. For this reason manufacturers rate their ropes not only for impact force but also for the number of falls they will take. The UIAA (Union Internationale des Associations d'Alpinisme) test at the moment requires ropes to be dropped with an 80kg weight with a simulated fall factor of 1.77, five times at five-minute intervals. The impact force on the first drop must not exceed 12kN. Needless to say ropes are designed to take a lot more than this, and the relevant technical specifications are enclosed with the rope when purchased.

Appendix 2
SELECTED CLIMBING VENUES

The following venues have been chosen to give an idea of some of the sites worth visiting in the UK. There are obviously thousands of places where you can climb, but these are some of my favourites, along with a couple of recommendations from colleagues. Hopefully you may visit some of these before too long, and enjoy the climbing as much as we have.

Crag/region:	Swanage
Guidebook:	*Dorset* Mark Glaister and Pete Oxley (Rockfax, 2005)
Description:	I have no qualms about putting this first, although this list is not in order of preference. I started my climbing career in Swanage – with a school friend and using my mother's washing line – and having survived that the only way was up! The cliffs are extensive, with the Subliminal and Cattle Troughs areas being good for the lower grades. It is a serious cliff, with most areas requiring you to abseil in, and care must be taken in high seas. However, it gives a huge variety of routes, climbable year-round.

The extensive cliffs of Swanage

Looking across Milestone Buttress, Ogwen Valley

Crag/region:	Milestone Buttress, Snowdonia
Guidebook:	*Ogwen and Carneddau* Iwan Arfon Jones (Climber's Club, 1993)
Description:	This is an atmospheric crag, home to a number of easy multi-pitch routes. Although it is getting a bit polished in places as a result of its popularity, it provides a great venue for learning about climbing longer routes. There are other crags nearby, with the impressive sweep of the Idwal slabs a short distance down the valley. In the other direction is Tryfan Bach, a great place for taking your first steps as a leader.

Crag/region:	Reiff, west coast of Scotland
Guidebook:	*Northern Highlands North* Various contributors (SMC, 2004)
Description:	This is a popular and attractive area, offering a huge variety of sea-cliff routes across the grade range. The area has lots of sections offering easy access to the base of the climbs, many in the lower grades. The climbable areas are extensive, with walk-ins varying from a few minutes to an hour or more.

Crag/region:	Wilton quarries, Lancashire
Guidebook:	*Lancashire* Les Ainsworth and Dave Cronshaw (BMC, 2006)
Description:	The Wilton quarries make up just part of the area covered by the guidebook. They provide a variety of climbs from easy through to very technical, on generally well-protected routes, with Wilton 3 giving the best range of lower-grade climbs. Wilton 1 is home to the prow, an imposing section of rock, harbouring a number of impressive and technical routes.

'Ann', E1 5b, Wilton 1

'Hy Brasil', VS 4c, Reiff

Climbing 'The Crucifix', VS 4c, at Crystal Slabs, Pembroke

Crag/region:	Pembroke, South Wales
Guidebook:	*Pembroke* John Harwood and Dave Viggars (Climbers' Club, 1996)
Description:	Pembroke offers a huge area of climbing, from easy climbs with simple access through to hard test pieces with swooping abseils needed to get to the bottom. The cliffs are very extensive, and range from single-pitch to longer multi-pitch routes. Part of the cliff area is under the control of the military at Range West, so access can be awkward there. However, there is so much more to occupy you that this collection of crags will keep you busy for a long time!

Crag/region:	The Tors, Dartmoor
Guidebook:	South Devon and Dartmoor Nick White (Cordee, 2000)
Description:	This large area of a random collection of crags allows you to climb rough rock on interestingly shaped tors in some very esoteric locations. Dartmoor is a very evocative place, and the climbing seems to reflect that. Both leading and top/bottom roping are common, and the area has some excellent bouldering on offer. Although areas around Haytor can be busy with tourists, there are plenty of other places where you can be on your own – unless you want to hear cameras clicking behind you as you climb!

Evening light at Hound Tor, Dartmoor

Crag/region:	Fairhead, Northern Ireland
Guidebook:	*Fairhead* Calvin Torrans and Claire Sheridan (MCI, 2002)
Description:	The spectacular expanse of the Fairhead cliffs offers 3 miles of excellent quality climbing. Known for its short walk-ins and placement-friendly routes, it offers climbs across the grade ranges, all with spectacular seaward views to north and east. If you're after solitude it's easy to find it here, and the sheer volume of routes will keep you going for years.

Crag/region:	Sandstone outcrops, East Sussex
Guidebook:	*Sandstone – South East England* David Aitchison-Jones (Jingo Wobbly, 2000)
Description:	The various outcrops that make up the southern sandstone area are a haven for those in the southeast of England. They provide the only climbing in the area and, in general, provide excellent sport. One main issue is that – almost without exception – the venues require you to either top/bottom rope or solo; leading is not an option due to the soft nature of the rock. Take care to protect the rock at the top, and always extend ropes over the edge to avoid erosion.

(Opposite) **Bottom-roping on East Sussex sandstone – 'Abracadabra', 5a**

Appendix 3
GLOSSARY

Abseiling (rappelling, rapping) To descend the rope, usually after the completion of a climb, often using a system of protection for safety. It will most often be carried out in order to reach the bottom of a climb or to retrieve gear.

Aid The direct use of equipment to help get up a section of a climb. This may be a single move, perhaps pulling on a sling or standing in a loop hanging from a wire, or a series of continuous moves for some considerable distance.

Alternate leads (leading through, swinging leads) Used in a multi-pitch situation, where one person will climb a pitch, belay, and bring up the second person, who will then become the leader for the next pitch, and so on.

Arête An outside corner.

Artificial route One that has been placed between others and may not take a logical line. Alternatively a route where the guidebook states that the use of certain features, maybe a crack line, is not permitted.

Back bar The long bar opposite the gate of a karabiner. The karabiner will be at maximum strength when a load pulls along the line of the back bar.

Back-clipping Where a leader clips a karabiner, most often on an extender, in the incorrect manner. It is important that the rope from the belayer comes up to the back of the karabiner and out through the front. This is so that when the leader moves on and up, the karabiner and extender keep the correct orientation. If it is back-clipped – the rope goes into the front and up and out from the back – there is a chance that the rope could unclip in the event of a fall, or the extender become undone from the bolt.

Bail out To come down from a climb before it is completed. This may be because it is too hard, the weather has changed or darkness is approaching.

Barn-dooring To pivot or swing off a hand- and foothold, due to being off balance.

Beer towel A traditional piece of kit used to wipe mud or dirt off the soles of boots prior to climbing. Obtained from a sympathetic local hostelry.

Beta To have knowledge of a route prior to climbing it. This is usually only of relevance to those climbing the highest grades, where having beta (or not) will affect the ethics of their ascent.

Bombproof Used to describe a running belay or anchor that is extremely good and able to hold almost any load. To have a 'bomber' runner on a route is to have a good, safe piece of protection in place, very helpful for the confidence of the leader.

Bottom-roping A method of rigging the rope where the belayer stands at the bottom of the crag. The rope will run up the cliff, through a couple of karabiners that act as pulleys, then back down the route to the climber. Very popular with group climbing sessions and outdoor centres.

Bulge A section of rock that protrudes outwards, away from the main section of rock. Sometimes only a few centimetres in size, larger bulges can be quite tricky to surmount. A bulge need not be overhanging, as it can occur on a slab or other off-vertical surface.

Buttress A large area of rock, often supporting many routes and usually of a pitch or more in height.

Chimney A wide crack in the rock, usually large enough for the climber to get inside, which can be climbed by methods such as back-and-footing or bridging. Chimneys receive little sunlight and so can be damp and slippery.

Chockstone A piece of rock jammed into a crack or chimney. A small chockstone can be very useful, as sometimes a sling used as a runner or anchor can be placed around it. Alternatively they can be huge – the size of a car or bigger – and may present the climber with a problem, possibly the 'crux' of a climb.

Choss A collective term for grass, twigs, leaves and mud. A 'chossy' route is one that is quite dirty and possibly unpleasant.

Corner The opposite to an arête, a corner is akin to the angle made by an open book.

Crater To hit the ground after a fall.

Crux The hardest section of the route, usually only for a move or two.

D-shape karabiner These have a pronounced curve at either end of the back bar. This allows the load to sit in the best position possible, in line with the back bar.

Dead rope The rope that comes out from the belay device which the controlling hand holds on to. Letting go of the dead rope means that control over the climber will be lost, so should never be done whilst he is on a route.

Deep-water soloing (DWS) 'Solo' climbing over the sea or a lake. Deep-water soloing is a serious pursuit and should not be undertaken lightly. Long falls into water do not make for a soft landing, and many DWS routes are on climbs where contact with rock on the way down is a real possibility.

Direct belay The type of belay where the total load will be taken by the anchor in the event of a fall. An Italian hitch clipped to a sling around a boulder is a good example of a direct belay.

Double rope A method where two ropes are used, each being clipped into separate runners. This gives enhanced security, important for those operating at the higher grades.

Free climbing Climbing without resorting to aid tactics. Free climbing is often confused by non-climbers with soloing, which does not involve the use of any ropes or other safety devices at all.

Friction climbing Using the friction of the rubber on your boots and the skin on the palm of your hands to make progress. Friction climbing confidently takes a lot of nerve; the more nervous you are the less your boots seem to want to stick! Often the only way up a 'slab'.

Gripped To be terrified to the point of not wanting to let go of a hold.

Ground fall potential A route or move where a slip could cause the leader to hit the ground. Any route with a ground fall potential should sensibly be avoided, or gear placed appropriately to reduce any possible risk.

HMS karabiner (pear-shape karabiner) These have a wide curve at one end, making them suitable for use with an Italian hitch.

Hanging corner/arête/chimney Indicates that the feature, a chimney for example, does not reach all the way to the ground or belay ledge, but is suspended out over the rest of the route.

In situ Equipment that is already in place on a route. It may be a sling, a piton or other piece of kit. Any gear found *in situ* must be treated with caution, as it will probably have been there for some time, possibly suffering from UV degradation, rusting and other detrimental factors.

Leading on Where the same person will be leading the entire route on a multi-pitch climb.

Leading through (alternate leads, swinging leads) A technique on a multi-pitch route where the person who has just seconded one pitch becomes the leader for the next.

Live rope The rope that comes out of the belay device and runs straight to the climber.

Lob Term used to describe a leader falling some distance.

Lower-off A leader descending when being lowered by the belayer. This may be, for instance, from a piece of gear when 'bailing out', or from the top of a climb when bottom-roping.

On sight A style of ascent seen as being the best and purest, where the route is climbed at first attempt and with no falls, practice or beta. Much aspired to by those climbing at the very highest grades.

Overhang A section of rock hanging over the rest of the route. This is a general term and could describe a 'roof', 'bulge' or large 'overlap'. Getting through an overhanging section of ground can be very tiring, and climbs will often avoid the problem by going left or right as appropriate.

Overlap Often a feature of slabs, an overlap is where one section of flat rock appears to be sitting on another, presenting a small roof that needs to be surmounted.

Pear-shape karabiner Another name for HMS karabiners, and good for use with an Italian hitch.

Piton A metal pin or peg that is knocked into a crack in the rock with a hammer. These are sometimes found *in situ* and are best left in place. If you are going to clip one, treat it with caution as rusting could have reduced its strength.

Pumped To be totally tired, usually in the forearms. This is often the result of hanging on too long or too tightly, and will require a short period of rest or 'shaking out' to remedy.

Ramp A section of rock that makes its way up, often diagonally, like a short or narrow slab.

Rap Short for rappel, and an alternative to abseil.

Redpoint A style of ascent that is completed after practising sections of a climb before linking them together, sometimes taking many months,. Only really relevant at the highest grades where to 'on sight' a route would be very difficult indeed.

Roof An overhanging section of rock, sticking out at 90° to the vertical. Often smooth underneath, a roof could be small or of considerable size. Presenting a real challenge to climbers, a route with a roof will either avoid it by going around the side, or will take it direct, perhaps by climbing a crack splitting it in some manner. This latter option is usually reserved for climbs of a high standard, although climbing over a small roof can sometimes be done at an amenable grade.

Runner Common name for a running belay, an anchor placed by the leader through which the rope can move freely and protect him in the event of a fall.

Screamer Delightful name describing a very long leader fall.

Screwgate A type of karabiner with a locking sleeve or automatic mechanism that can be fastened to prevent accidental opening. Common on main anchor systems and key running belays.

Scoop A rock feature that looks as it sounds, frequently with smooth sides. Not deep enough to be a chimney, a scoop is a gouge, often vertical, out of the rock. Sometimes quite small, a scoop can also be huge, perhaps a pitch or more in height.

Semi-direct belay The 'usual' method of belaying when climbing, where the belay device is clipped into a rope loop at the harness, and so the load is shared by the belayer and the anchor.

Shaking out The action of resting the arms after becoming tired or 'pumped'. The climber drops his arms down to his side and shakes them gently in order to help reduce the effects of lactic acid that will have built up during the climb.

Slab A section of rock leaning back from the vertical. The ascent of a slab may well rely on 'friction climbing', and might offer little in the way of cracks for protection.

Snapgate Karabiners that do not have a locking mechanism on the gate. These are used extensively for clipping gear when leading, as they can be employed very quickly and effectively.

Soloing To climb without ropes or other protection,

with the understanding that a mistake could have serious, and quite possibly fatal, consequences.

Sport climbing A popular style, where all of the protection is *in situ*, in the form of bolts drilled into the rock. with hangers that are then clipped with an extender.

Spotting Looking out for the safety of a climber when he is near the ground, often prior to clipping the first runner. Spotting is most usually done by the second, who will be in a braced position with arms outstretched, ready to field the climber should he slip. The idea is not to catch the climber but to keep him on his feet and prevent him from falling backwards and tripping over a hazard.

Stance The area from where belaying takes place. If on a multi-pitch route it will be called an 'intermediate stance'.

Swinging leads The same as leading through or alternate leads.

Top out To complete a climb by getting to the top of a route and up over the edge. The most usual style of finishing, it gives a real sense of achievement and, for most, is what climbing is all about.

Top-roping A system of rope control where the belayer is positioned at the top of the crag (the opposite to bottom roping). This allows a climber to complete an entire route and 'top out'.

Traditional climbing The ascent of a route where all of the protection equipment is placed by the leader. This is different to sport climbing, where the leader clips extenders onto *in situ* bolts drilled into the rock.

Twin rope A technique where two ropes are treated as one, with both clipped into each runner. Differs from double roping, where each rope is clipped into separate runners.

Wall A section of rock rising vertically.

Working a route Spending time on a climb, trying to sort out each individual move and practising everything. Often a precursor to a redpoint ascent.

Z-clipping Where the rope from below the last piece of gear is clipped into the one just placed. This is dangerous and could subsequently involve the gear being pulled out and the leader being faced with the potential of a long fall.

Zawn A gash in sea cliffs leading right down to the water. Often a 'V' in section, a zawn can make traversing a crag difficult, as any cliff-base ledges will usually be missing.

INDEX

The main reference is in **bold**.

iNDEX

LISTING OF CICERONE GUIDES

AFRICA
Climbing in the Moroccan Anti-
Atlas
Kilimanjaro
Trekking in the Atlas Mountains

THE ALPS (Walking and Trekking)
100 Hut Walks in the Alps
Across the Eastern Alps: The E5
Alpine Points of View
Alpine Ski Mountaineering:
Vol 1 – Western Alps
Vol 2 – Eastern Alps
Chamonix to Zermatt
Snowshoeing: Techniques and
Routes in the Western Alps
Tour of Mont Blanc
Tour of Monte Rosa
Tour of the Matterhorn
Walking in the Alps

EASTERN EUROPE
High Tatras
Mountains of Romania
Walking in Hungary

FRANCE, BELGIUM AND LUXEMBOURG
Cathar Way
Ecrins National Park
GR5 Trail
GR20 Corsica
Mont Blanc Walks
Robert Louis Stevenson Trail
Rock Climbs Belgium and
Luxembourg
Tour of the Oisans: The GR54
Tour of the Vanoise
Trekking in the Vosges and Jura
Vanoise Ski Touring
Walking in the Cathar Region
Walking in the Cevennes
Walking in the Dordogne
Walking in the Haute Savoie:
Vol 1 – North
Vol 2 – South
Walking in the Languedoc
Walking in Provence
Walking in the Tarentaise and
Beaufortain Alps
Walking on Corsica
Walking the French Gorges
Walks in Volcano Country

GERMANY AND AUSTRIA
Germany's Romantic Road
King Ludwig Way
Klettersteig – Scrambles in
Northern Limestone Alps
Mountain Walking in Austria
Trekking in the Stubai Alps
Trekking in the Zillertal Alps
Walking in the Bavarian Alps
Walking in the Harz Mountains
Walking in the Salzkammergut
Walking the River Rhine Trail

HIMALAYAS – NEPAL, INDIA, TIBET
Annapurna
Bhutan
Everest

Garhwal & Kumaon
Kangchenjunga
Langtang, Gosainkund and
Helambu
Manaslu
Mount Kailash Trek

ITALY
Central Apennines of Italy
Gran Paradiso
Italian Rock
Shorter Walks in the Dolomites
Through the Italian Alps: the GTA
Trekking in the Apennines
Treks in the Dolomites
Via Ferratas of the Italian
Dolomites:
Vols 1 and 2
Walking in Sicily
Walking in the Central Italian
Alps
Walking in the Dolomites
Walking in Tuscany

NORTH AMERICA
Grand Canyon and American
South West
John Muir Trail
Walking in British Columbia

OTHER MEDITERRANEAN COUNTRIES
Climbs and Treks in the Ala Dag
(Turkey)
Crete: the White Mountains
High Mountains of Crete
Jordan – Walks, Treks, Caves etc.
Mountains of Greece
Treks and Climbs Wadi Rum,
Jordan
Walking in Malta
Walking in Western Crete

PYRENEES AND FRANCE/SPAIN
Canyoning in Southern Europe
GR10 Trail: Through the
French Pyrenees
Mountains of Andorra
Rock Climbs in the Pyrenees
Pyrenean Haute Route
Pyrenees – World's Mountain
Range Guide
Through the Spanish Pyrenees:
the GR11
Walks and Climbs in the
Pyrenees
Way of St James – France
Way of St James – Spain

SCANDINAVIA
Pilgrim Road to Nidaros
(St Olav's Way)
Walking in Norway

SLOVENIA, CROATIA AND MONTENEGRO
Julian Alps of Slovenia
Mountains of Montenegro
Walking in Croatia

SOUTH AMERICA
Aconcagua

SPAIN AND PORTUGAL
Costa Blanca Walks:
Vol 1 – West

Vol 2 – East
Mountains of Central Spain
Walks and Climbs in the Picos
d'Europa
Via de la Plata (Seville to
Santiago)
Walking in the Algarve
Walking in the Canary Islands:
Vol 1 – West
Vol 2 – East
Walking in the Cordillera
Cantabrica
Walking the GR7 in Andalucia
Walking in Madeira
Walking in Mallorca
Walking in the Sierra Nevada

SWITZERLAND
Alpine Pass Route
Bernese Alps
Central Switzerland
Tour of the Jungfrau Region
Walking in Ticino
Walking in the Valais
Walks in the Engadine

INTERNATIONAL CYCLE GUIDES
Cycle Touring in France
Cycle Touring in Spain
Cycle Touring in Switzerland
Cycling in the French Alps
Cycling the River Loire – The
Way
of St Martin
Danube Cycle Way
Way of St James – Le Puy to
Santiago

MINI GUIDES
Avalanche!
Navigating with GPS
Navigation
First Aid and Wilderness
Medicine
Snow

TECHNIQUES AND EDUCATION
Adventure Alternative
Beyond Adventure
Hillwalker's Guide to
Mountaineering
Hillwalker's Manual
Map and Compass
Mountain Weather
Moveable Feasts
Outdoor Photography
Rock Climbing
Snow and Ice
Sport Climbing

For full and up-to-date information on our ever-expanding list of
guides, please check our website:
www.cicerone.co.uk.

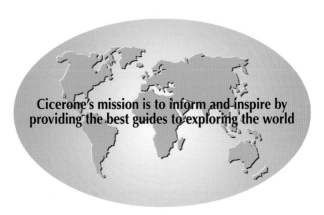

Cicerone's mission is to inform and inspire by providing the best guides to exploring the world

Since its foundation over 30 years ago, Cicerone has specialised in publishing guidebooks and has built a reputation for quality and reliability. It now publishes nearly 300 guides to the major destinations for outdoor enthusiasts, including Europe, UK and the rest of the world.

Written by leading and committed specialists, Cicerone guides are recognised as the most authoritative. They are full of information, maps and illustrations so that the user can plan and complete a successful and safe trip or expedition – be it a long face climb, a walk over Lakeland fells, an alpine traverse, a Himalayan trek or a ramble in the countryside.

With a thorough introduction to assist planning, clear diagrams, maps and colour photographs to illustrate the terrain and route, and accurate and detailed text, Cicerone guides are designed for ease of use and access to the information.

If the facts on the ground change, or there is any aspect of a guide that you think we can improve, we are always delighted to hear from you.

Cicerone Press
2 Police Square Milnthorpe Cumbria LA7 7PY
Tel:01539 562 069   Fax:01539 563 417
e-mail:info@cicerone.co.uk   web:www.cicerone.co.uk

CICERONE